Wild Soundsc

REVISED EDITION

WILD SOUNDSCAPES

DISCOVERING THE VOICE
OF THE
NATURAL WORLD

BERNIE KRAUSE

Yale

UNIVERSITY PRESS

New Haven and London

Published with assistance from the foundation established in memory
of Calvin Chapin of the Class of 1788, Yale College.

Yale University Press books may be purchased in quantity for
educational, business, or promotional use. For information, please
e-mail sales.press@yale.edu (U.S. office) or sales@yaleup.co.uk
(U.K. office).

Set in Adobe Garamond and Gotham type by
Westchester Publishing Services, Danbury, Connecticut.
Printed in the United States of America.

ISBN 978-0-300-21819-0
Library of Congress Control Number: 2015956508
A catalogue record for this book is available from the British Library.
This paper meets the requirements of ANSI/NISO Z39.48-1992
(Permanence of Paper).

10 9 8 7 6 5 4 3 2 1

For Kat, always

Contents

CONTENTS

Sound examples indicated by ⟿ are available at
yalebooks.com/wildsoundscapes

Foreword

I have always preferred radio to television, agreeing with the old saw that in radio "the images are better." Back in the 1970s I encountered a wonderful example of that. One summer's night I found myself out late in Algonquin Park in Canada. We were howling at wolves—trying to record them. Although we got a single very faint answer from a distant wolf, it was not what we wanted; the rest of the recordings from that evening were just the local ambient natural sounds, including the trickle of a nearby brook, some crickets, and a distant wood thrush that was up later than usual, singing its final evening vespers.

During a hard snowstorm in the following winter, I was searching through some tapes for whale songs when I happened upon a tape that was marked with a note saying it had nothing on it and was reusable. I couldn't imagine what it was, so I put it on. There was the distant wood thrush in his acoustic surrounding: its recorded song instantly transported me back to the summer evening in Canada. The sounds created a flood of feeling, lifting me out of my winter surroundings and setting me down in the midst of hot summer. I can even remember feeling warm, for a moment. This was accomplished more strongly than I would have imagined possible, even though the outside world was frozen clean through its heart. It was a powerful lesson, demonstrating to me that sounds are more evocative than any other sense, even more than the sense of smell, where subtle whiffs of familiar odors—such as the smell of grandmother's house—are able to bring back vivid memories from past decades.

Bernie Krause apparently feels the same way. He notes in this interesting and useful book: "When [recorded sounds are] at their best, nothing in the human-created visual world, by itself, even comes close to their impact." He tells the story of when he recorded a jaguar that had followed him through the Amazon jungle one night; after he set up his recording gear and moved a few feet off, the jaguar came silently up to his microphone, sniffed it and then made a low growl. As Krause points out, a photograph of such an event might cause you to smile nervously, but listening to the recording of the jaguar sniffing and growling makes the hair on the back of your neck stand up. Krause includes this recording in the audio web site for this book, and you are unlikely ever to forget it—it is utterly chilling. When you listen to it, ask yourself if any moving image has ever evoked such an intense response in you.

Because of the evocative nature of sound, Krause regrets that so few people have either the equipment or the knowledge to record the sounds that would, when listened to later, transport them back to places and situations they have loved, and do it better than pictures ever can. One of the most useful parts of the book describes how to get equipped at a reasonable cost. For this he recommends connecting with a proactive online community of recordists from around the world to help with these decisions at any level of experience. He also describes some of the tricks of the recording trade.

The most important point made in *Wild Soundscapes* is that it is not the single, dissected-out, cleanly recorded voices of nature that transport you back most vividly to the places where, and the times when, you recorded them. The best "beaming up" occurs only when such voices are embedded in their own acoustic surroundings—what Krause refers to as their biophonies and geophonies (*biophonies* being the voices of living things, and *geophonies* being the non-creature sounds of the earth, such as thunder, rain, and wind).

Biologists such as Krause and I focus on recording natural soundscapes to secure the experiences we wish to relive later, but he emphasizes that all soundscapes, whether natural, urban, or rural, possess extraordinary evocative powers. His thesis fights a hard battle; like the photographs in one's family album, no outsider is ever as moved as the person who took them, just as some may not be as moved by a recording as the person who was at a site and recorded its marvelous sounds. Yet I urge you to take Krause at his word: go out and buy the equipment for making your own recordings, and record ambient sounds whenever you are in places you wish to remember. And do this until you are as reflexive about making such recordings as all of us are about taking pictures whenever we find ourselves in places we wish to remember. Krause is right: ambient sounds will get you back to such a place more vividly than any photograph ever can . . . and they will do so more effectively than you can imagine.

Krause also explores how non-industrial cultures have always depended "on the integrity of undisturbed natural sound for determining a *sense of place*." He cites the Babenzélé (Ba'Aka) Pygmies who live in the Central African Republic, as an example. When separated from the forest, these people "become physically and mentally stressed and overwhelmed." Krause claims that "natural soundscapes are a physical and spiritual elixir." In contrast, he discusses our noisy modern world as exemplified in the crowds who are drawn to drag races by "the power of noise." He notes, "The louder the sounds we can produce, the more virile we are supposed to feel, absent anything else of consequence that provides us with a sense of self- or spiritual-worth."

Krause, like me, prefers it quiet. As he says, "Listening to creature sounds, water trickling in a stream, wind in the trees, and waves at the seashore immediately puts me at ease. . . . Yet this miraculous biophony—this concerto of the natural world—is now under serious threat of complete annihilation." He makes a strong plea for the critical importance of conserving the acoustic integrity of such places. I predict that this book will become an important voice in support of preserving natural soundscapes.

There are chapters encouraging novice sound recordists to discover unusual things to record, such as singing sand dunes or barnacles moving inside their shells. For those who get caught by the recording bug, he suggests grand projects, such as following the route of Lewis and Clark's journey from St. Louis to the Pacific, recording all the way. Or perhaps a recording trip that acoustically follows the seventeen-hundred-mile journey of Chief Joseph of the Nez Percé tribe, beginning in northeastern Oregon, over the Lolo Pass in Idaho, south through the Bitterroot Valley, across Yellowstone and ending at the Bear Paw battlefield in Montana near the Canadian border. It is difficult to imagine a better way to satisfy a twin interest in history and the outdoors. This is a new way to think about planning a vacation.

There is also a useful section on troubleshooting the problems you will encounter with field recording equipment. His final, excellent advice to someone whose equipment has completely broken down and can't be fixed: "Take a deep breath and enjoy the view. Electronic equipment fails sometimes." Other practical advice includes the admonition never to use insect repellent containing the chemical DEET because "it dissolves everything."

Wild Soundscapes features a wonderful section about where to go to record lovely natural soundscapes. It includes such interesting details as a great place to see a specific pack of wolves, as well as an aside on President Reagan's infamous remark, "If you've seen one redwood, you've seen them all." Krause's experience points to just the opposite. Traveling all over the world to record, and comparing the sounds he has been able to capture, Krause says, "They all sound different . . . if you've heard one beach, you've (only) heard the unique geophony of one beach."

We are late in being able to understand the natural world through sound. Krause points out that, until quite recently, we had no way to store or reproduce sound. Thanks to the more artistic of our cave-dwelling ancestors, we know what woolly mammoths looked like eons ago. If those same ancestors had been able to record sound, we would also know what they sounded like. Imagine experiencing a recording of a woolly mammoth trumpeting in the forest outside the cave. What an evocation of a distant time and place.

What Krause's book is calling for is a whole new way of interpreting our world. For that reason and many others, this is a book I recommend you buy, read, and act upon.

Roger Payne

Wild Soundscapes

Learning How to Listen

White camellias
falling—
The only sound
in the
moonlit evening
—*Ranko*

The day I arrived here two weeks ago the meadow was wrapped in a blanket of snow. Now I sit amid sprouting wildflowers, listening as small rivulets of water etch delicate traceries through the melting crystalline patches that remain along the forest's edge. Birds are beginning to nest on the newly exposed grasses—the Lincoln sparrows are so unruffled by my presence that I move about freely without upsetting any of the settled females. Everywhere, there are nests full of eggs swathed in tufts of grass and among the low brush and trees that surround my campsite. I feel like a kid again: hopeful, trusting, full of dreams. Listening like this engages me totally with a sensation of heightened awareness and peace, just as it did many years ago. I wait a while, seduced and intoxicated by the divine ensemble that envelops me. Only then do I think to fire up my recorder hopefully to capture on tape the resonant biophonies that reach my ears. Streams, like their marine counterparts, the rivers and oceans of the world, are among the most difficult natural sounds to capture so that they appear true-to-life when played back; more often than not, these transformed sounds seem nothing like the pure, radiant expressions that we sense by mere listening. I've spent the last several days capturing just the right aural perspectives to mix into a soundscape composition that might evoke this charmed location. My ears have become so attuned to the serene natural world that when I think of returning to the city, I can only imagine a din of noise. It is the same almost every time I journey into the field.

—*Journal entry, Lincoln Meadow at Yuba Pass,*
California, 15 June 1988

This book centers on an intimate engagement with the natural world: learning to read and capture the collective acoustic expressions of living organisms from wild habitats. The first edition, published in 2002, was a compilation of the known field listening and recording practices of the time. The original idea grew out of the visitor soundscape manual the National Park Service commissioned me to write just after the turn of the millennium.[1]

Over the course of the past dozen years the subjects related to soundscape ecology and interests in field recording have exploded. Now there are many ways of considering natural soundscapes. Among them are their integration into private and academic collections, scientific curricula, and various forms of expression through the lenses of the humanities—a crucial synergy between science and the arts.

This book addresses ways we might learn to listen to and capture many of the multiple sounds that our ears detect—otherwise known as *soundscapes.* Soundscapes, in turn, are made up of three basic acoustic sources. The first is the *geophony,* or non-biological natural sounds that occur in natural habitats. The second general source includes the special collective voices of the natural world—those that

I call the *biophony*. Increasingly, these voices are becoming difficult to find, yet if we wish to better understand our connection to the natural world it is essential that we find ways to experience these acoustic expressions, and preserve and protect the habitats where they remain vital and intact. A major reason some of those biophonies are obscured or lost to us is a result of the third acoustic source—one that is human generated. I call that source *anthropophony*. These terms will be fleshed out in more detail in subsequent chapters.

Wild Soundscapes is not a guidebook or instruction manual in the traditional sense. Most guidebooks provide detailed descriptions of trails and paths, and depict the flora, fauna, and terrain of an area that you plan to visit. They focus on the physical features one is likely to encounter by *sight*. This book is a resource for exploring new ways to experience the fundamental messages of the natural world through listening and interpreting natural sound. There is not a beginner or a longtime professional I know who does not learn something new each time he or she ventures into the field. That's because the discipline itself is still in its infant stages. What is called "soundscape ecology" gained a reputation as a separate subject in just the last twenty years. In general, though, we are lucky because the topic is supported by a number of really helpful online global communities with many members who have been more than willing to share their hard-won knowledge without judgment. Some of these communities are highlighted at the end of this book.

By trying out some of the exercises and learning to interpret the significance of the sounds you hear, you may discover that your overall perspective of the world changes dramatically. That was certainly my experience. Without fail, new insights reveal themselves every time I record. I have designed these exercises to help you distinguish those sounds that are particularly useful to you and informative. Use the glossary at the end of the book for terms you don't know. Come up with new ones and share them with the community. Skip around to sections that most interest you. Use the sound examples, indicated by the icon 🎧 and located at yalebooks.com/wildsoundscapes, to hear some of the sounds I've described.

No matter how you approach this text, you will gain fresh insights into many aspects of the soundscape. You will learn new skills that enable an understanding of sonic events, many of which will help to fine-tune your listening capabilities.

Don't be intimidated. You won't need fancy technologies or, for that matter, any technology to engage with natural soundscapes. You can experience the collective voices of the natural world simply by savoring them with your ears alone. That said, this account will also enable you to enhance and expand your ability to listen and decode natural soundscapes through the use of intuitive, inexpensive, and accessible recording gear.

When I first heard natural sound enhanced by a microphone and a pair of earphones, in an urban wooded area north of San Francisco nearly half a century ago, the impression was so overwhelming and resonant that I completely lost track of time and was oblivious to the approaching night. Finding myself alone and apprehensive in an unfamiliar world, I stumbled down what were otherwise well-marked trails without a flashlight, finally reaching the spot where I had parked my car. It was my first experience venturing alone into what I naively had thought of as wild territory, and I was embarrassed by how little I knew of my environment and its extraordinary inhabitants.

Ironically, our awareness of natural soundscapes is one of the last frontiers of discovery in the biological sciences. Since the evolution of vocal organisms on earth, aural niches have been understood and put to practical application by many traditional cultures. In our scientific and humanities literature it is only in the past century that initial inquiries were made considering the implications of this phenomenon as an issue of importance. So we are quite late in coming to an understanding of the natural world through sound and have to relearn how to listen in the ways our ancestors did tens of thousands of years ago if we are to decipher its rich and informative narratives. However, for those of us who wish to learn new listening skills, the timing could not be better; new discoveries in the field of soundscape ecology are being made almost every day. Sites filled with critter sounds are thrilling to explore. Major breakthroughs are sure to follow as we learn more about our multiple and interdependent links to them.

Throughout this text I use the term *natural world*, rather than *nature*, when speaking of the landscapes from which the collective voice of creatures and the habitats emanate. *Nature*, an overused and abstract word, has become intertwined with Western symbolism creating an "it/us" dichotomy and separating humans from the very subjects we are attempting to describe. Many cultures that live more closely linked to the natural world do not have a single word for nature. For those and many other reasons, the term will be used sparingly throughout this text.

I need to digress for another moment to convey what I mean by "wild." A paraphrase of Bill McKibben's ideal definition works best for me. He tells us that a wild place is one where you can walk for a week in any direction and not encounter a road or a fence. It's a place with no signage or rangers eager to explain the life cycle of a moose, a grizzly bear, the bald eagle, or a pine marten. And, best of all, there's nothing to buy.

As my passion to listen to and record acoustic events expanded, I quickly discovered there were no resources to guide me; outside of traditional musical terms, there are few words in American English to describe the phenomena of sound in general, and natural sound-scapes in particular—and no specific historical or cultural precedent to value them. Now, after several decades of working in the field as a naturalist and soundscape ecologist, I have learned a few tips I want to share that might help. Mostly, I want to impart my craving for this work and my observations about what the natural world is telling us. It is critical that we pay attention to those messages. So while you are having fun acquiring new listening skills, you will also get some new insights about creatures, their habitats, and how human noise impacts our experience of the natural world.

The first time I heard a spring dawn chorus picked up by my microphones and transmitted through headphones, the feeling made me realize that with my ears alone, I had been missing exquisite parts of the experience. Amplified sound gave me a way to interpret the language of the natural world in ways my "civilized" ears, trained to hear as a professional musician, could not possibly grasp. First, I had to recalibrate my hearing so that I could hear biophonies with something approaching what our forest-dwelling ancestors might have known. Those special voices of life reached me with an impact so great that my world was forever transformed: *heightened listening was the key.*

Many of us do not distinguish between the two acts of listening and hearing. As the saying goes, it is one thing to hear—quite another to be able to listen. The first obstacle I had to overcome in my learning curve was my inability to do just that. Although my ears *heard* sound, they were not trained to distinguish the many subtleties present in more wild settings. Listening through headphones and microphones gave me a tool to attend more carefully.

Microphones amplify sound in certain concentrated ways and focus our attention, enabling us to listen more critically. They let you differentiate between what to listen *to* and what to listen *for* in much the same way that a microscope or a pair of binoculars can increase your ability to focus on, identify, and observe details in the visual realm. Through a good pair of headphones, you hear pieces of the aural fabric in such clear detail that you will be amazed by all that you have previously missed. You will also become more cognizant of things to avoid that interfere with our experience of still-wild places, such as the sounds of barking dogs, lowing cows, and the omnipresent human mechanical domain.

Learn to listen in an *active* rather than a passive way. A keen awareness of and involvement in the fascinating dominion of living sound can be achieved by anyone willing to learn how to become a *careful* listener, and the joy of learning is so gratifying! Living sound surrounds us. Our awareness of it intensifies our bond with vocal organisms and makes us better able to flourish in our chosen environments. Nevertheless, the natural world is slow to reveal its secrets, and few of us are trained to listen with the kind of attention needed.

For most of us living in the midst of modern industrialized cultures, hearing has become a blur. As much of the world population shifted from agrarian to industrial economies, the local folk soon realized their aural environment was being transformed: railroads and factories drastically altered the land- and soundscapes, and we bent our lives to the age of the machine and all the noise that the era has brought with it. Noise, in this instance, is defined as incoherent and chaotic acoustic signals that transmit no inherent information or intelligence. Anthropophony—at least the incoherent and chaotic part—is generated, in large part, by the ruthless, careless pace we force upon ourselves and is expressed largely through our technologies.

(Stuart Gage, an emeritus professor from Michigan State University, has suggested replacing *anthropophony,* meaning human-created sound, with the term *technophony,* because humans generate a lot of sound through the use of their technology. While the term is an excellent one, my guess is that it fits as more of a subclass of anthropophony, because humans also produce a lot of sound that isn't technologically based. So the larger field would embrace *all* human-generated sound, rather than just the technically produced.)

In recent years, noise has increased exponentially in our living and recreational environments and now permeates and masks many of the more aesthetically resonant sounds. One result of increased noise levels is a surge in the level of stress detected in many organisms—including ourselves. Over time, we have partially adjusted to the acoustic complexities and higher volume of our environment and learned to endure a culture of noise, but it left many of us seriously listening-challenged, hearing-impaired, sick, or even tone deaf to those very elements that might otherwise enrich, nurture, and soothe us. There is even evidence that humans living in societies where there is little human-induced industrial or mechanical noise have a far smaller incidence of health and hearing problems.[2]

We have come to endure a type of experience in the natural world akin to going to a movie whose subject follows one plot, while the sound conveys another, conflicting story. For instance, the sounds of snowmobiles in Yellowstone National Park completely obliterate the serene peacefulness otherwise present during the winter months. It is as if our civilization dispensed with natural soundscapes as a vital part of our experience—as if it doesn't matter or exist at all. You would never think of going to a movie theater that is outfitted with an advanced surround sound system and turning off the sound during a performance. Why should it be different with our experience of the natural world? The encounter with natural sound adds a vibrant and palpable dimension to our visual experience.

The first time you experience the natural world's creature choruses through techniques and tools described in this book, you might be bewildered by the seemingly disorganized and unexpected quality of the sound. What seems chaotic at first is generally the result of our inability to comprehend the complex patterns that biophonies reveal. Stephen Jay Gould, the Harvard evolutionary biologist and popular science writer, has suggested that human beings have great difficulty grasping larger, more complex concepts even when they may hold the keys to simpler truths. We have a situation where "the invisibility of larger contexts [is] caused by too much focus upon single items, otherwise known as missing the forest through the trees."[3] Sound comes to us in a combination of both fixed and variable manifestations simultaneously. Robins will always sing in my backyard in the spring: the constant. This is an established, predictable event that my wife, Kat, and I hear, every year. However, they sing from different trees, in varied numbers and from diverse positions with each passing day: the variable. They likely do this because the natural world constantly scans for optimum transmission and reception of signals, sending out its messengers like the American robin, to verify the results. Because our experience of listening to wild soundscapes is so new, at this point we know very little about what these creature sounds impart. Nevertheless, by training ourselves to listen more attentively, we can all begin to "read" these indicators within a larger, holistic context as they start to reveal themselves.

I can't imagine a life without the nourishment of the wild soundscape's divine music enveloping me. Enjoying and finding comfort in this wild symphonic performance has had a major impact on me; it has led to many marvels and satisfying insights, a sense of peacefulness, and certainly a more healthy lifestyle. This book is an effort to bring those miracles into your world. As you learn to listen, you will be able to transform the everyday moment-by-moment experience of your life and benefit in a number of unanticipated ways.

So many urban situations directly increase apprehension, with noise level being chief among the culprits bringing about anxiety, panic, hyper-sensitivity and general nervous tension. On the other hand, the sounds of the creature world, of water trickling in a stream, wind in the trees, and waves at the seashore, immediately put us at ease. Most of us relax and slow down when we disconnect ourselves from the noise of cities, smartphones, iPads, and ever present electronic media. We breathe more deeply, take in more oxygen, reinforce our sensory apparatus, and replenish our frayed neurons. At some point, many of us recognize a deep need to proactively support the preservation of tranquility and work to protect natural soundscapes wherever they remain intact. Thus, the popularity of rain sticks, meditation retreats, living room water fountains, and well-produced natural sound recordings.

The kind of active and considered listening I propose is quiet, meditative, and gentle. It is designed to create a new understanding, a collaboration between kindred spirits, human and Other, discovering the ways in which we all make our presence known. If we select the right places to patiently listen and wait, we might find that the creature world has stories to divulge that are nothing short of amazing. As our understanding and connection to the natural world increase, it is my hope that we will be moved to learn about, preserve, and protect the divine voices of these vulnerable habitats.

1

The Mystery of Sound

With the sense of sight, the idea communicates the emotion,
whereas, with sound, the emotion communicates the idea, which
is more direct and therefore more powerful.

—*Alfred North Whitehead*

Of all the human senses, hearing is the most mysterious.
R. Murray Schafer once wrote, "I have never seen a sound." Because
sound is so elusive, it has relatively little worth in this culture. What
is the value of the original *Mona Lisa* compared with a performance
of a Bach Prelude, where one object can be held in the hand and
the other cannot? And although we can experience acoustic signals,
they are nearly impossible to define. Yet what we hear in wild places
is not only fascinating and immeasurably rich in detail, but absolutely vital to our lives and our survival. Nothing can replace it.

The ear is a magical receptor, capable of processing far more complex information than we had ever thought possible. Through the
operation of the ear and the brain together, we are linked to information we may never fully comprehend. Nevertheless, we must keep
in mind that every natural soundscape is a proto-symphony that reveals a detailed and powerful narrative across a very wide range of
disciplines. Now is the time to decipher it.

Sound, because it is so intimate, immediate, and physical, is probably the most influential of our senses: if loud and persistent enough and of a certain quality in a given space, it can actually cause the temperature there to rise. Think of all the knowledge and emotion communicated through the medium of sound. It can inform or elevate us, make us feel sad, inspired, or soothed. It can terrify us, as in the sounds of war or a natural disaster. Or it can create in us a sense of serenity, and evoke a wide range of mental images.

Sound is also key to much of our entertainment: try watching *Star Wars* with the sound track turned off. That is what you would actually "hear" in space (nothing). But complete silence makes us feel utterly uncomfortable and disoriented. Imagine a world without Bach or Beethoven, Lightnin' Hopkins or Miles Davis, or Peter Gabriel. However, the use of loud sound design to create excitement or suspense, or to represent action and drama, often leads to such acoustic agony in some quarters that even the loudest wild creature's voice is drowned out. We are even learning that some sounds, such as prolonged loud and distorted noise, can actually cause serious illness and, in some cases, even death. On the other hand, it is encouraging to note that a growing body of research is now being done on sounds that heal.[1]

What Is Sound?

Sound is the sensation that comes from electrical signals in our nervous system's auditory center. But this is not where this sense begins. A movement, whether a beating wing or the vibration of skin on a drum head, produces pressure waves in the air molecules around it. These waves then travel through the air at a high enough rate (frequency) and at a high enough level (amplitude or loudness) for our ears to detect. Our ears translate the waves, once received, into impressions. The extraordinary and complex mechanism of the human ear allows us to discriminate between extremely fine details in the texture of sound. Even many of us with some hearing impairment can distinguish the sound of one human voice from another. Just as we have an innate ability to distinguish between individual human voices, we also possess a latent aptitude that allows us to hear patterns among less familiar voices, such as those expressed in the natural world. These creature voices define the status of habitats within certain environments and can provide new insight into our experience of the wild.[2] As civilization has become industrialized, it has effectively dismissed the ability to hear the natural soundscapes in discriminating ways. We are now a visual culture—informed largely by what we see. The focus of this book is to learn, once again, to use our auditory gifts in conscious ways more balanced with the rest of our senses. It is a process of discovery both wonderfully informative and a joy to encounter.

Two Types of Sound

Desirable and undesirable sounds are differentiated in the field of bioacoustics as those that convey useful *information* as opposed to *noise*. We're often not mindful of the noise that surrounds us, what the author Joachim-Ernst Berendt refers to in his book *The Third Ear* as "acoustic garbage," when hearing with our ears alone. Yet our brains are at work filtering out undesirable sounds so that we can better hear and process what is beneficial or useful—information that we might need to have.

We have all had the experience of attempting to talk with a companion in a noisy restaurant or on a crowded urban street. As we gaze at the source of the sound, we think we are hearing everything perfectly. However, our hearing is aided mostly by *what we see.* In our auditory centers, we are receiving many sounds, but our brains are at work filtering the background noise and making us think that the background interference doesn't matter. This activity goes on whether or not we are fully conscious of it. But we are simultaneously subjected to varying degrees of measurable fatigue and stress even as our attention is focused on what we see, with our brains functioning overtime to retrieve and process the desired information.

Some businesses manipulate this process in order to trigger or reduce human stress levels. Restaurant architects and interior designers, for example, plan restaurant environments to be more or less stressful. There's a practical reason: By introducing hard, reverberant surfaces that reflect and amplify the slightest sound, they can create a noisier space. The noise triggers stress and fatigue responses that encourage quick patron turnover, resulting in higher profits for the restaurateur. Consider how relaxed you feel in a quiet eating establishment with lots of sound-absorbent material factored into the design—and how less likely you are to hurry out the door. The *New York Times* discussed the problem of restaurant noise in a number of editorials several years ago; subsequently, it began to report noise levels as part of its regular restaurant reviews to give readers appealing and quiet options. The *San Francisco Chronicle* places small bell icons in restaurant reviews to identify a restaurant's noise levels, and many other newspaper and magazine food critics follow similar models.

The presence of unwanted noise becomes most apparent when we introduce a microphone into the equation. Microphones, an extension of our ears, do not discriminate between useful sounds and noise. They pick up *every signal* within the limits of their design and pattern. If you want to know how much noise there is in an environment, just plug a mic into a recorder and put on a set of headphones.

Try recording a particular habitat. Select an environment that is familiar to you. Bring along a stereo microphone and recorder and hit the "record" button. Focus on something as simple as a conversation in a quiet part of your home without background noise (such as refrigerators humming, entertainment centers buzzing, telephones ringing, cars passing outside, dogs barking). Or, try a place outdoors, such as a neighborhood park or footpath. Play back your recording when you return home. After this experience, your way of listening will begin to change.

Research on Noise

Since the early 2000s, there is more funding for new research on noise and its impact on human and other organisms and there is a great deal of interest in the subject—particularly in Europe. However, the area of study that has attracted the greatest amount of attention has focused on the relationship between extremely high decibel exposures and hearing loss. One indicative study, linking noise and stress, took place in the early 1980s in Strasbourg, France. Researchers invited three young men and three women to sleep in a specially designed laboratory where they were subjected to different sound and noise experiences each night over a period of several weeks. Wired to stress-level instrumentation that registered heart rate, finger-pulse amplitude, and pulse-wave velocity, each test subject was monitored throughout the night. They were first introduced to a few nights of uninterrupted quiet, followed by two weeks of recorded traffic noise. All of the stress indicators dramatically increased when the traffic noise was first introduced. Upon waking, participants completed questionnaires detailing their experience.

After two to seven nights of noise, the subjects reported that they were no longer aware of being disturbed. Each person had become used to it. However, the physiological stress levels measured by the instrumentation showed the same consistently high numbers as noted the first night when the traffic sounds were introduced.[3] Although the minds of the subjects rationalized that there was no noise issue, their bodies told a very different story.

What Is the Soundscape and What Are Its Component Parts?

The *soundscape* is the acoustic structure of any environment, whether urban, rural, or natural. It includes all of the acoustic signals that reach your ear at any one time from all sources. Undisturbed natural soundscapes, places where no human noise is present, often feature a glorious symphony of creature and non-creature voices. As human clamor increases and habitats shrink, non-human sounds have become difficult to hear or muted altogether. Animal survival often depends on the numerous ways in which creatures vocalize in their particular habitats. When unwanted noise occurs, human and non-human creatures alike are denied an experience of their important acoustic connections. Humans especially lose that positive interaction between themselves and the living world. In the next chapter, we will further explore just what creature soundscapes are and how we can recover our links to them.

The concepts of *soundscape* and *acoustic ecology* were first brought into our common language by R. Murray Schafer in a book titled *Tuning of the World*. In another piece, *Je n'ai jamais vu un son* [I

Never Saw a Sound], Schafer reminds us of one of our own creation myths:

> God spoke first and saw that it was good second. Among the creators, sounding always precedes seeing, just as among the created hearing precedes vision. It was that way with the first creatures on earth and still is with the new-born babe.

Acoustic ecology, an older term that first appeared during the World Soundscape Project conducted at Simon Fraser University in Vancouver, British Columbia, in the late 1970s, is a field of study concerned with the relationship between soundscape and listener and how this relationship characterizes the quality of any given urban, rural, or natural soundscape.[4] It is still the main focus of the World Forum for Acoustic Ecology. More recently, the International Society of Ecoacoustics, which convened for the first time in June 2014 in Paris, changed the focus of that inquiry to the narrower concept of soundscape ecology. The emphasis is a continuation of the initial work several of us began in the late 1990s with the study of sound across the entire landscape and the development of new terminology to define the acoustic phenomena being discovered nearly every day.

Loss of Natural Soundscapes

Natural soundscapes, particularly biophony and geophony, are no longer the primary indicators most of us use to gather knowledge about our environment. We tend to be suspicious and fearful of experiences in the wild—ones that we cannot easily explain or quantify—and we shy away from those conditions that we believe we cannot control or tame. There is a large-scale devaluation of natural soundscapes in particular because they are so elusive and require a certain amount of critical thinking to decipher—educational and philosophical models not currently emphasized in U.S. education—so we often become intimidated by such engagements.[5] Yet at some point in our distant past, we intimately knew the place where we lived as much by sound as by sight, scent, or physical texture. An awareness of our surrounding environments was required all of our senses. No single faculty dominated the others.

While human beings shifted from hunter and gatherer cultures to agrarian ones, we built villages and cities where we conducted trade and localized rites. As these urban centers around the globe became more populated, and humans began to travel widely, beliefs and attitudes about the natural world changed, along with our relationship to natural sounds and noise. Control over what we viewed as "nature" became essential, with humans self-referred to the apex of the power spectrum. Along with this first major change, domestic animals, waterwheels powering mills, blacksmiths pounding iron into various shapes, church bells summoning the faithful, and cart wheels rumbling over cobblestone streets altered the entire soundscape. These sounds confirmed for many certain social bonds and productivity. Pride in our accomplishments first peaked just after the Industrial Revolution, around the turn of the twentieth century, when we began to equate noise with advancements in civilization. As more human noise was introduced into our environments—cumulative signatures that masked natural sound—one of the most forceful reminders of our connection to natural-world phenomena began to recede into memory along with a nagging sense of loss often expressed by writers and poets of the time.

Sometimes, when a bird cries out,
Or the wind sweeps through a tree,
Or a dog howls in a far-off farm,
I hold still and listen a long time.

My world turns and goes back to the place
Where, a thousand forgotten years ago,
The bird and the blowing wind
Were like me, and were my brothers.

My soul turns into a tree,
And an animal, and a cloud bank.
Then changed and odd it comes home
And asks me questions. What should I reply?
—*Hermann Hesse, "Sometimes"*

As population centers grew during the intervening centuries, a large-scale alteration of natural areas into agricultural production began to radically transform the landscape. Another major shift in attitude occurred with the achievement of our illusory summit within the hierarchy of the living world. Philosophical attitudes toward the natural world shifted away from the reliance on wild habitats as civilizations grew in social and economic complexity. Almost imperceptibly at first, with each passing century and at an exponential rate, more land went into production with little sense of or regard to the limits of the natural resources being transformed. Parallel with this change, attitudes about still wild habitats also became more distorted and were expressed through worry and alienation as we became increasingly separated from our atavistic roots. Interpretation of religious doctrine in the West held that "Nature" was, indeed, something to be dominated and subdued. To my mind, that included the "wild" (read: creative) in human nature, as well. Music, meant to lionize aspects of the natural world, also reflected those anomalies through multiple contradictions, although that may not have been the composers' intent.

By the end of the fifteenth century, Savonarola, a monk-dictator living in Florence, concluded that the tritone, an interval of an augmented fourth in the musical scale, was "the Devil's music." The Catholic church deemed some types of sound offensive, while it condoned other types of musical sound and styles. Many intellectuals of the time found great spiritual significance in the "music of the spheres," considered to be the harmonic sound made by the rhythm of the planets and stars as according to a divine plan and also a Pythagorean speculation on the relation of whole numbers to musical consonances.[6] However, it's my guess that the natural world of which we are but a small part had other ideas.

Dominance of the Visual

Until quite recently, we have had no way to store or reproduce natural sound. Visualization of the living world, on the other hand, has been represented since the Paleolithic period. More than 30,000 years ago, humans discovered that they could capture the image of a gazelle or a mammoth on cave walls deep in the earth. Our perception of the natural world changed and has diverged in numerous forms of representation and abstraction ever since. The graphic image became a powerful force in our understanding of real and mythological worlds. Wherever those images were created, many attained divine status.

Sound was different. Because our visual sense was the only one we could technologically reproduce up until the mid–nineteenth century, when Léon Scott de Martinville invented a sound recording device in France (1857) and Thomas Edison created the first phonograph (1877), we favored our other senses. Much of human culture, particularly as our civilization developed in the West, has historically been based on the physical information we gain from the *visually observable* cues. Most of the sciences have historically emphasized visual observation and abstraction as the most faithful method of perceiving and explaining our domain. In addition, many of our valued art forms also place their greatest emphasis on what can be seen or touched.

Balancing Our Senses

As we strayed from the more balanced use of our senses within the natural world, our ability to listen in the discriminating ways of our ancestors was seriously modified. Many years ago, I had the good fortune to spend time in the Amazon Basin with the Jivaro, an indigenous tribe that thrives in the wild much as they have done for several thousand years. My experience with the Jivaro helped reorient my thoughts about the powers inherent in natural sound and gave me some insight into what many of our ancestors once knew about hearing and understanding their verdant habitats.

One evening, when I was invited to join the men of the tribe on a traditional hunt, we traveled under the forest canopy without flashlights, torches, starlight, or moonlight. There was nothing to direct us except the biophony. Guided only by oddly shaped acoustic grids of finely partitioned and collective choruses composed of nighttime birds, mammals, insects, and amphibians, we made our way through otherwise unseeable territory.

I was hearing only a frenzied din; yet those who knew how to listen to biophonies heard the same chorus as an exquisitely defined narrative jam-packed with everything they needed to know about the moment and their objectives. The distinctive patterns of the forest voice guided the hunters in the general direction of their prey and eventually helped pinpoint the game's location. Surrounded by complete darkness, the hunters knew what creatures lurked down the path and whether or not the organisms were prey worthy of the hunt or threats to be avoided. The forest soundscape itself served as a finely gauged GPS for them, with the added advantage that they could also interpret the vast quantities of aural data much the way a skilled sightless human navigates urban territory.

As I stumbled through the rainforest that night, it struck me that we had experienced a tremendous loss when we turned to the world of the visual for our most important cultural imprints while dismissing sound. At that moment I became determined to relearn some of the skills that my fellow humans living in the Amazon forest still held sacred.

Recovering the Precious

The late Pitzer College ecologist Paul Shepard argued that we are still connected to that ancient voice of the forest or desert. He suggested that the human genetic code has not changed since we emerged as *sapiens* from the Pleistocene.[7] Our studies of indigenous cultures like those of the Jivaro, the Babenzélé (Ba'Aka) Pygmies in the Central African Republic, the Kaluli of Papua New Guinea, and the Pitjanjatjara of the Australian outback inform us about the relationships these groups have to the soundscapes of their respective territories. All four demonstrate remarkable similarities in the ways they connect to wild habitats and living sound; it is from them that we may learn to hear faint echoes of our own sonic past.

By the year 2000, it was becoming apparent to me that natural soundscapes furnished not only the roots of language but the foundation of music as well; long before we began to worship the power of pictographs and petroglyphs, the animals in our desert and forest environments taught us to dance and sing as we mimicked and shadowed their graceful movements and voices. However, if we wish to hear creature orchestras again, we have to slow down, become very quiet, and listen intently. Perhaps we even need some new technologies to enhance our experience and retrain our ears. Of all the issues surrounding natural soundscapes, none is more urgent than finding tranquility through the reduction of unwanted noise that permeates nearly every habitat, an issue that will be addressed in more detail in Chapter 7. For now, I'd like to explore the power of natural world soundscapes and their various component parts.

2

Stories Revealed by the Biophony

Any living thing which triumphs in the struggle against its environment destroys itself.

—*Gregory Bateson*

There was a time when we were able to read the stories embedded in natural soundscapes in much the same way as those histories are now related in books. This delicate acoustic fabric is as well defined as the notes on a page of music, especially when viewed as spectrograms. The notion that there can be a profound effect on soundscapes by the introduction of human-induced noise has long been understood by non-industrial cultures that depend on the integrity and guidance of undisturbed natural sound for a sense of place, as well as for spiritual and aesthetic reasons. In fact, the very physical and mental health of more earth-centered cultures, the soles of whose feet are in frequent contact with the ground, depends on the special relationship between the undisturbed biophonies and geophonies of their respective habitats.

John Muir once wrote of an encounter with soundscape narratives in the Sierra Nevada. Sitting alone in a grove of white pines, he was captivated by the singular winglike drone of pine needles whirring in the wind. He claimed he could tell where he was by the sound of the needle vibrations alone, even if he were set down blindfolded anywhere in that vast range.[1] It is this method of distinctive listening that we need to reacquaint ourselves with.

Historically, researchers in the natural sciences abstracted single components out of a larger context in an effort to better identify, quantify, and categorize individual elements and organisms. The first students of natural sound practiced the same method, which brought some elements to light. However, it's my conviction that much more can be learned by listening to the *collective acoustic signals* expressed within an entire habitat. The density, diversity, and richness of biophonies collected from whole habitats always convey more robust information than can be revealed by any single element—at least to my ear.

I was formally educated in the classical manner of scientific and cultural deconstruction. This kind of reductionist fragmentation taught me to segment the components of the natural world into its various parts. I learned how to distinguish one species from another, and to pay particular attention to the sounds of single members of individual species. Yet to truly understand the relationships between components, I recognized early on that without a more inclusive perspective, a vital dimension of the picture was missing; I realized that the collective voicings of entire habitats contained a far more complete package of information.

Academic literature has rarely focused on the notion of the aural interdependence of vocal organisms in a given habitat. Nevertheless, the idea was toyed with. In a paper in 1977 on birdsong, Peter Marler and Kenneth Marten suggested the possibility that creatures vocalize in some (yet to be understood) relationship to one another.[2] In another publication, Jakob von Uexküll, a behavioral physiologist of the early twentieth century, referred to the notion of sensory niches in general.[3] According to some historians of the field, this work is considered seminal.

I will never forget my delight when, in 1987, I first became conscious of what later became known as biophony.[4] While re-evaluating the recordings I had done in Africa four years earlier, it became apparent that the sounds on tape were more ordered than I had originally thought. At first, I simply heard what I thought were frequency-related patterns. Then, with the aid of emerging sound analysis software, it became clear to me that the phenomena also included temporal niches as well. The many different creatures expressing themselves through sound, it turns out, are using very specific frequency ranges and time patterns, or niches in the dense web of sound. The differentiation in their patterns most likely evolved over a long time, and it allows members of each species to communicate with other individuals as well as with other species.

I referred to this idea as "the niche hypothesis," a phrase suggested by my colleague Ruth Happel. What most of us had formerly considered a chaotic din consisted instead of a cohesive set of sounds, made up of all the vocal creatures in a particular habitat, with their voices structured in relation to one another over both frequency and time. Furthermore, the patterns convey not only aspects of the physical history of a habitat but a great abundance of other information, as can be seen in graphic illustrations of sound called *spectrograms* (figure 1). The spectrogram illustrates approximately ten seconds of recorded sounds, reading left to right. The scale on the right side depicts the frequency range in hertz (Hz), or kilohertz (kHz), from lowest at the bottom to highest at the top. (A *hertz* is a unit of frequency defined as one cycle per second. A kilohertz is one thousand hertz.) The relative amplitude (loudness) of each sound is indicated

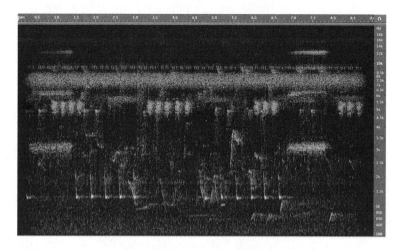

1. Spectrogram of the dawn chorus in a thriving habitat
at Camp Leakey, Borneo

by the darkness or lightness of the patterns (the whiter the pattern,
the louder the sound, and vice-versa).

A clear example from a specific habitat can be found in a recording of a complex tropical biophony from Camp Leakey, Borneo, made
in March 1991, and its associated spectrogram. The sounds heard on
the recording and represented in the spectrogram from Camp Leakey
show a healthy, relatively undisturbed habitat. The sound patterns
reveal a diversity, density, and discrimination of voices that are quite
distinctive, and consistent with a long-established, healthy ecoregion or biome. The patterns demonstrate clear niche differentiation,
which was likely established over a considerable evolutionary period,
where large numbers of creatures occupy various frequency ranges
and times.

Two horizontal lines—a thick one between 7 and 8 kilohertz (kHz),
and a thin one above it at 9 kHz—represent insect vocalizations.

Within the dark areas, where there is otherwise no other vocal energy, you can see three kinds of birds, including a chestnut-winged babbler *(Stachyris erythroptera),* which calls four times at around 5 kHz, and a Malaysian eared nightjar *(Lyncornis temminckii)* at approximately 1.4 kHz, which vocalizes in a succession of notes in two separate clusters. A cicada appears two times in three different frequency niches (approximately 3 kHz, 6.5 kHz, and 12 kHz) simultaneously. Cicadas must have taken a very long time to learn a vocalization that fits so neatly into three niches of the audio spectrum, and this quite possibly provides a way of measuring the habitat's age.

Another sound example is from Pic Paradis, a mountain located on the French side of Saint Martin, an island in the Caribbean, recorded in 1986. It exemplifies a relatively newer-growth environment, having been previously clear-cut in the 1950s.

Insects occupy a bandwidth in one niche, which appears as a thick horizontal line between 3.5 and 4 kilohertz (figure 2). The frog spectrum appears as another wide horizontal band between 2 and 2.5 kHz. At dawn, when this recording was made, two species of birds filled niches where there was little or no interference from other sounds. A mourning dove *(Zenaida macoura)* sings four times (showing up as four lines, like dashes, toward the bottom center of the image at around 500 Hz). The second bird in the sample is a pearly-eyed thrasher *(Margarops fuscatus),* which can be seen in the abrupt vertical lines jutting above and below the insect band.

As the spectrogram shows, the biophonic pattern in this recording is relatively light in both density (the total number of vocal organisms) and diversity (the total number of different vocal species). This is because the habitat has not fully recovered from its earlier deforestation in the 1950s, even though this recording was made

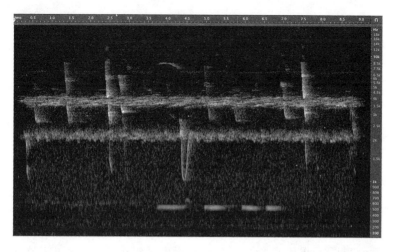

2. Spectrogram of the biophony in secondary-growth biome
at Pic Paradis on Saint Martin, Virgin Islands

some thirty years later, in the spring, in a subtropical island habitat, when vocal density is normally much greater. The elaborate acoustic fabric once there is no longer present, partly as a result of habitat loss and intense development, and partly because of the noise generated by human populations that now permeates the entire area.

When we compare the wilder environment with an altered one (even though I do not mean to equate similar types), we begin to see the impacts of deforestation through the differences in both density and diversity expressed through the biophony.

Human Impact on Biophonies

Since 1984 I have been listening to and recording spadefoot toads (*Spea intermontana*) around Mono Lake just east of Yosemite National Park. What is so splendid about toad chorusing is the way one critter begins and others soon join in. After a while, they all join together in a way that forms a synchronicity of sound that absolutely engulfs and hypnotizes you. A couple of years ago, I was able to capture a direct correlation between human-induced disturbances to the toads and their defensive response. The incident involved a low-flying military jet over the Mono Lake basin in April 1993, one evening while my wife and I were camping and recording.

Many types of frogs and toads tend to vocalize together, so no individual stands out among the many, which functions as a kind of acoustic camouflage. This chorusing creates a protective audio performance that confuses predators and keeps them from locating any single point from which an organism vocalizes (figure 3). The frog voices emanate from so many places at once and are so much in sync that they appear to be coming from everywhere. When a loud noise, such as a jet plane flying overhead, disturbs the amphibians, the special frog choral synchronicity is broken. While they attempt to reestablish the unified rhythm and chorus, individual frogs momentarily stand out. This gives predators, like coyotes, foxes, and owls, a perfect opportunity to snag a meal.

In this case, as the flyover is occurring, the number of creatures vocalizing declines, and there are breaks in synchronicity at approximately 2.5, 3.5, and 4.5 seconds (figure 4). After the jet disappeared, forty-five minutes passed before the toads were able to reestablish their full chorus. During that time, under a full moon, we watched as two coyotes and a great horned owl began feeding by the side of the small pond. Because of the unique manner in which we record and measure sound, we have discovered that the relatively intense noise produced by a low-flying jet aircraft can cause changes in the biophony.

Another aircraft flyover, in February 1990 at a research site called Kilometer 41 in the Amazon Basin north of Manaus, Brazil, illustrates

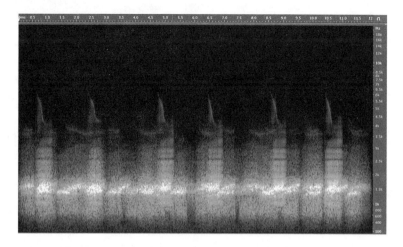

3. Spectrogram showing the protective multivoice chorus of spadefoot
toads at Mono Lake, California

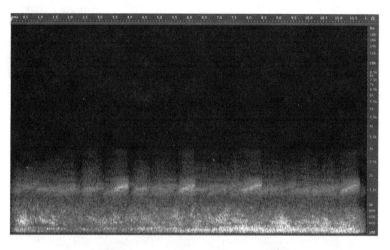

4. Spectrogram of the spadefoot toad chorus being interrupted
by a low-flying fighter jet

the first noise-related incident we were able to both capture on tape and show graphically. Listening to the dawn chorus one morning, Ruth Happel and I recorded a low-flying multiengine military jet as it shattered the jungle soundscape. Just moments prior to the arrival of the jet, there are finely delineated and discriminated features of the biophony present that can be both seen and heard (figure 5). When the jet passes by, the effect on the biophony is dramatic (figure 6). The creature voice discrimination recovered, but it was several minutes before it returned to normal.

No one knows for certain what types of human mechanical noises effect changes in the behavior of wild creatures; there are likely too many permutations. We do know that noise directly affects *our* experience of wildlife. When I am in the field trying to get the acoustic feeling of a particular site, most human noises will distract me and often affect the behavior of the creatures I'm there to see, hear, or record. I am aware that even my own presence can have an effect.

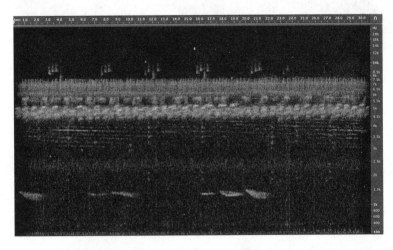

5. Spectrogram of normal daytime biophony at Kilometer 41 in the Amazon Basin, Brazil

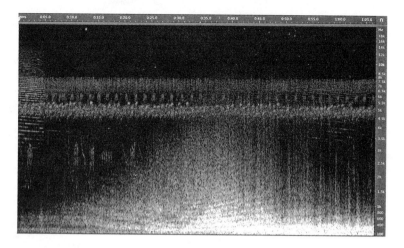

6. Spectrogram of the biophony disrupted by a low-flying multiengine jet, Kilometer 41, Brazil

Many visitors to our national parks have expressed similar concerns. But it is not always the loudness of a sound that causes animals to bound over a ridge out of sight or to become silent when in the presence of an intrusive mechanical device. Sometimes it's the quality or character of the sound, referred to as *timbre* in music. The flyover of a Piper Cherokee 140 (a single-piston-engine private plane) may have a far different effect on certain creatures than an F-16 jet, even if both are measured at the same level of loudness. It largely depends on an organism's perception of the threat level and what the timbre of the signal represents.

In the late 1970s, while working on my doctorate, I served my internship in bioacoustics on a research vessel observing humpback whales in Glacier Bay, Alaska. We watched as the whales tried to swim away and hide from the noise introduced into their marine environment from passing cruise boats. The whales would duck behind spits of land or small icebergs broken off from glaciers in an effort to find quiet shadow zones. Whale numbers in the bay were declining in the late 1970s, when research supported by the National Park Service was under way; where once there had been many, fewer and fewer were found by 1978 and 1979. Trying to pinpoint the cause, some researchers cited increased tourist vessel activity as a likely culprit. Taking into account other factors such as variations in krill populations (tiny shrimplike creatures that are a major component of the humpback food supply), and the special manner in which certain vessel noise may be amplified by the geological features of the bay contour, the consensus was that boat noise was still the major contributing ingredient to the falling numbers.

On the other hand, just south of the bay's entrance in Icy Strait, and to the east in Frederick Sound, humpback populations continued to thrive during the summer months despite large numbers of boats of all sizes and levels of noise output. While this does not mean they are unaffected by the noise, rarely have the whales been observed swimming away from boats in these areas. Humpbacks feed in these waters during the short Alaskan summer months and must increase their body weight substantially prior to their reverse migration to Hawaiian waters. To some extent, habituation to the noise is essential to their survival. The effect of measurable stress levels induced by human noise in humpbacks of this region is yet to be determined. Nearly every time I have dropped a hydrophone (an underwater microphone) in Icy Strait to record the wonderful humpback feeding sounds, I am amazed by the amount of propeller noise generated by commercial and private watercraft that can be heard as far away as eight miles. Yet the whales keep on feeding, playing, and vocalizing. Over a period of fifteen years and as many trips, I have successfully recorded a total of three or four minutes of whale feeding vocalizations (sometimes called "contact sounds" because they seem to lure other whales to the vicinity of the singer) without anthropogenic noise interfering. The seductively exuberant sound during those few minutes when the ambient marine environment was absent human noise was truly unforgettable.

The biophonies of special places change as a result of human intervention. Forests are a good example. A couple of miles east of Yuba Pass on the Sierra Nevada mountain ridge line north of Truckee, California, Lincoln Meadow was once a pristine edge habitat replete with a wide variety of spring birds, insects, and amphibians. A selective logging operation one summer in the late 1980s completely transformed the soundscape, as we will discuss further in Chapter 12.

When researchers consider the effects of human-induced noise as a factor in biophonic loss, the results are notable because there is not much attention being paid to how animals or their respective habitats might be affected. From my experience and that of many visitors to the national parks, the introduction of noise into natural soundscape heightens that sense of loss.[5] During my work in the field, I have also noticed a wide variety of changes in creature behavior, demonstrating possible stress when a chainsaw fires up or a snowmobile or a straight-piping motorcycle approaches.

Because human and non-human species respond differently to types, loudness, or combinations of mechanical noises, we are beginning to understand that many of these sound types introduce distress in all animals even though the victims may not *seem* conscious of or act in response to the cause. For example, the elk herds in Yellowstone are experiencing a fair amount of measurable stress as a result of certain kinds of mechanical noise. In the spring of 2001, Scott Creel, a biologist at Montana State University, along with a number of his colleagues, reported a link between snowmobile noise and elevated glucocorticoid (stress) enzyme levels in elk and wolves in the wild populations in Yellowstone and Voyageurs National Parks. During the period of time that snowmobile traffic increased 25 percent, there was a 28 percent increase of stress levels in wolves. Conversely, within Voyageurs National Park, a 37 percent decline in snowmobile traffic between 1998 and 2000 correlated to a drop of the same percentage in stress enzyme levels in wolves. Comparable figures were found in elk populations.[6] Although the study concluded that the stress levels appeared to have no impact on the population dynamics of either the elk or the wolves, it failed to take into account aberrant behavioral effects similar to those we've noticed with spadefoot toad populations. The noise level in Manhattan, Rio de Janeiro, Paris, or Jakarta seems to have no effect on human population dynamics, either.

Once lost, biophonies in the state and range of their original dynamic equilibrium are unlikely to be reestablished. Over 50 percent of North American biophonies archived in my library have been collected from whole ecoregions now altogether silent or so radically altered that the they can no longer be heard in any of their original forms. No one will ever be able to hear the voice of these environments at their bioacoustic peaks again, except as recorded. They are sites forever transformed. Yet there are rays of hope. Late in the game, we are beginning to understand that vital natural soundscapes are precious treasures and resources critical to our enjoyment, understanding, and awareness of the natural wild, especially the knowledge of our own history. Without these biophonies, a fundamental piece of the fabric of life is sadly compromised.

Another hopeful sign of change is visitor reaction to the noise in the national parks. Visitor surveys conducted by the National Park Service in the early 1990s convinced the agency that it is important to attempt to hear and treat soundscapes differently, that they are as crucial to the overall well-being and health of the parks as the preservation of pure fresh water, clean air, and non-polluted soil. Indeed, there was once a plan in place to phase snowmobiles out of Yellowstone National Park altogether. Tourist overflights over Rocky Mountain National Park were eliminated. Flights over the Grand Canyon had been limited to some extent. However, there is a countervailing "wise use" movement that advocates for expanded private property interests and commercial activities on public lands, which leads to serious concerns about the manner in which these environmental policies can be effectively implemented. If the park service succeeds in convincing the visiting public of the importance of this noise-free model, the idea will certainly spread, and we will have progressed toward a more responsible stewardship of our wild public lands.

In the early 2000s, the National Park Service had the insight and the momentary power to designate natural soundscapes as a *resource*. Made under the political radar, the mandate provided that the park system decree that natural soundscapes would be protected with the same levels of vigilance as the protection of wildlife, streams, woodlands, and meadows. Along with the ruling came the implementation of a strong educational and administrative program to introduce visitors to the enjoyment of natural soundscapes as part of the wild park experience.[7] Soundscapes within the parks were momentarily valued and deemed worth preserving for visitors and creatures alike. This marvelous program was one that any visitor could take to heart because of its simplicity and importance. (And it served as the model for the first edition of this book.) Sadly, the program was put on hold in 2004 because of political pressure from a few characters in Congress who were convinced that the term *soundscape*—derived from landscape and seascape—was too "radical." As a result, the park service's Natural Soundscape Program, which we worked hard to implement for research purposes and for the many direct benefits provided to visitors, was subsequently renamed the Natural Sounds Program. Outside of this book, the program has been all but abandoned and leaves no direct visitor legacy.

To my mind, nothing heals the spirit and body more completely than the incantations of biophonies. To reconnect to the potent sonic elixirs found in our remaining wild soundscapes, we must pay new attention to the sonic world, and adopt new, more comprehensive methods of discerning the information we hear. In other words, we need to think of and value natural sound in constructive ways. Despite our past and entrenched training, it is exhilarating and revealing to learn to listen to the voices of *whole* environments as structured and informative narratives and to discover what they can tell us as we begin to explore the natural world with more attentive and open ears.

3

Exploring Soundscapes

A wilderness exists in man that refuses to be studied.

—*Loren Eiseley*

In the mid-1980s, I began taking clients on listening and recording sound safaris to places like Alaska, Costa Rica, Australia, and Africa. I wanted to introduce folks to the world of exhilarating sound in areas where they could experience pristine soundscapes. For several years I concentrated on the inland and coastal ecoregions in southeastern Alaska around Chichagof Island, south of Glacier Bay and directly across Icy Strait from the mainland (figure 7).

This area consists of a wide variety of coastal marine and terrestrial habitats that clients especially enjoy. It is a transitional coastal subarctic temperate region with widely variable conditions. In summer, there are short, five-hour nights, while daytime temperatures can at times reach into the high seventies or low eighties Fahrenheit. It can also be quite cool and wet. It's Alaska!

As part of each workshop, participants were asked to join in a number of exercises designed to heighten their awareness of what they heard. First, they were instructed to concentrate on what they experienced with their ears alone. The group identified habitats, natural occurrences, and creatures by the unique sounds they encountered.

7. Yakobi Island, which sits just off the western end of Chichagof Island in southern Alaska

Each day we explored a different type of environment, noting its acoustic characteristics during wet and dry weather, the best ways to listen, what was heard, how sound changed with weather or time of day or night, and what creature or non-creature sounds made up the texture of the soundscape. We also explored the best ways to capture these soundscapes as recorded documents.

This is a list of biomes that the participants considered and were asked to describe:

- muskeg, or bog
- coastal coniferous forest
- marsh
- lake (shoreline)
- bay (inner tidal zone)

- riparian (fast and slow water zones)
- inland coniferous forest
- open marine environment (with whales, seals, birds, and airborne voices)
- submarine environment (underwater voices of fish, whales, seals, crustaceans)
- tide pool
- ocean shoreline.[1]

The following is a list of non-biological sounds, or geophonies, that one group identified:

- rain
- wind (not recordable per se—only its effects as it blows across broken reeds, through the upper stories of trees, and so on)
- streams, both fast and slow running
- different types of lake, ocean, and inland waterway wave action
- glacier masses moving over land
- glaciers crackling (as ice melts)
- glaciers calving.

The group was then charged with putting together a list of critter sounds they heard. It included four species of whales, bear, wolves, two types of seals, sea and river otters, sea lions, anemones, barnacles, seventy-four species of birds, plus snapping shrimp and even fish. Along with recording, this listing exercise provided a great deal of supportive information about a habitat's health. Because we were in a northern transitional zone, we heard only a few insects— mosquitoes mostly.

When participants compared the biophonies of two or more environments, they were ultimately able to identify their location by biophonic signatures alone. In one coastal coniferous zone the group heard and recorded varied thrushes, Swainson's thrushes, the ubiquitous white-crowned sparrow, ruby-crowned kinglets, robins, marbled murrelets, bald eagles, red-tailed hawks, mourning doves, ospreys, yellow-rumped warblers, ravens and crows, and, aside from mosquitoes, an occasional bee. In this particular location, we also heard wolves one morning. Geophonic sounds included the effect of wind blowing through the canopy of the forest, waves lapping on the nearby shore, and water flowing in a nearby stream.

As the group moved inland a short distance to a small lake fed by a stream with a tiny waterfall at one point, the biophony immediately changed to include a mix of common loons, robins, American dippers, a great horned owl, a flock of herring gulls, hairy woodpeckers, and swallows. Here, we saw a river otter but it made no sound while we were present. Non-creature sounds at this location differed from the coastal coniferous settings by the nature of the gently flowing stream, a waterfall in the distance, and the tiny freshwater waves lapping on the shore, which are quite different in acoustic character from saltwater waves, partly, I suspect, because of a difference in density (saltwater is denser). In calm weather, freshwater waves tend to be gentler and more rapid in their repetition.

When we dropped a hydrophone into the water from our kayaks where we had paddled just offshore, we were able to hear the sounds of humpbacks bubble-netting, followed by their "contact" or feeding calls. We also heard snapping shrimp, and even some harbor seals. In a tide pool, we lowered the hydrophone into the mouth part of an anemone, which sucked it into the creature's belly, trying to digest it. Finding nothing of nutritional value, the anemone expelled the hydrophone with a hearty belch, backed by the biophony of barnacles twisting in their shells and tiny rockfish darting from shelter to shelter in the pool.

You can explore soundscapes wherever you happen to live. They exist in your own backyard, down the block, in an open field, in the hills behind your house. The pond in your city park might be as vibrant as more distant undisturbed sites. The trick is learning how to engage with them. It's easy. The following soundscape exercises will guide you.

In order to remember all the details and as a prelude to your field exercises, always have a notebook and a pencil or pen handy. (If you can't live without technology, bring a tablet, computer, smartphone, or some other device to make notes.) R. Murray Schafer suggests that we do the following: jot down five environmental sounds (not music) you've heard today that you like. Finally, name five sounds (not music) that you don't like. What makes these pleasing or not to you?

Now let's take an actual example of an activity that would bring all of this together in a general way no matter which trail or journey you choose. The objective is to listen in ways you may have never considered.

First find a quiet spot, one where there is no anthropophony of any kind but where there are only creature or natural sounds: a stream, a meadow, a lake, a favorite forest, a mountain, a beach, a muskeg. You may need to walk, bike, paddle a canoe or kayak, or ski to get there, but it's worth it. If you're near a city, you may not find a place that is completely quiet. However, there are *times* when noise is at a minimum, like very early morning (before dawn) or late at night. Remember that if you're driving to a seemingly remote spot, others can drive there too, and your location may tend to be noisy for that reason. If you happen to live in or near a densely populated area, seek out *noise-free intervals,* or NFI, defined as periods of fifteen minutes or more with no mechanical or domestic noise (dogs, cows, sheep, roosters) present.

Notice that I've made a distinction between *noise* and natural soundscapes. I consider noise to be any sound that intrudes, covers, blocks, or distorts the articulation of sounds coming from the natural (as opposed to domestic) creature world. Turn-of-the century wit Ambrose Bierce once defined noise as "the chief product and authenticating sign of civilization."[2] This has never been more true than today. Mostly, noise in the context of this book refers to undesirable human-induced or mechanical noises—the technophony, as Stuart Gage terms it. But those dogs, roosters, cows, and sheep can have the same effect on our experience when we're concentrating on biophonies produced by wildlife.

The dawn chorus, which happens just after first light and around sunrise, is usually the best time to listen because the bird vocal density is at its peak. This is true especially in the spring. Give this effort enough time and you'll discover that there is a special aural fabric unique to each particular location.[3] The sounds you hear at dawn, midday, afternoon, dusk, and nighttime may define the habitat more clearly and with more detail and clarity than any Ansel Adams photograph. To reach these theaters of biophony, don't hesitate to go some distance away from places where human noises tend to be greatest. (Of course, practical outdoor skills, such as good judgment, are essential.) You'll be rewarded with something sublime nearly every time. Throw away anything that reminds you of the time and allows you to text or take selfies. Let natural time and events define themselves by the waves of creature orchestrations. Consider several things while performing this exercise.

What do you mean by a quiet spot? What do you mean by noise? How does noise affect your appreciation of the wild (or anything, for that matter)? What types of natural sounds within a given environment make you feel good? Relaxed? Aware? Awesome?

Once we feel comfortable listening in discriminating ways, three basic conditions are required for sound to register in our minds. First, the sounds need to be within a range that humans hear—roughly 20 Hz to 20 kHz. Second, the sounds need to be loud enough so that we can detect what is being expressed (often noted in decibels, or dB, where one unit of change relates to the smallest shift the human ear can detect). Third, we need a reasonably good set of ears that have not been destroyed by high levels of urban or electronically produced noise.

The first two elements take into account much of the creature world, but not all. Many mammals have voices that fit neatly into the range of human hearing, everything from rodents (including mice and bats) to large megafauna like elephants and whales. However, there are certain bats and dolphins (small whales) that humans cannot hear unaided because their voices exceed the highest frequencies we can detect. In some cases, a particular creature's vocal range may partially overlap ours, extending higher or lower in pitch than what we are able to hear. Elephants and larger whales are included in this category. In fact, the highest-voiced creature in the mammal world is not a bat or an insect, but the blind Ganges dolphin (*Plantanista gangetica*), known to have a voice in excess of 250 kHz—nearly six octaves higher than the highest note on a typical piano. It is thought that one of the large whales possesses the lowest voice—around 4 Hz—although it is not known for certain which species. The fin whale (*Balaenoptera physalus*) has been heard to vocalize around 15 Hz. Elephants, giraffes, and possibly hippos have special contact vocalizations (vocal syntax that draws others to the vicinity of the "singer") lower in frequency than what humans can detect without the aid of some technology. Of the insect world, we can hear perhaps 20 to 30 percent of what exists. Many insects produce signals so high we cannot detect them, and many have voices too soft to hear unaided. In the avian world, we can hear most of what is represented, although the upper harmonics of some birds well exceed our ability to perceive them. In the amphibian world, we hear nearly all available sounds (except those voices expressed underwater). Some reptiles, such as crocodiles, produce some of their sounds at frequencies lower than what we can hear, but most can be heard within our normal range.

There are many voices the unaided ear cannot hear clearly in marine environments like lakes, ponds, oceans, and swamps. This includes marine insects, fish (near coral reefs in particular), anemones, whales large and small, shrimp, and barnacles (although at low tide, barnacles exposed on rocks sometimes rotate in their shells and emit a high clicking sound). Sounds become muffled underwater, and we do not hear them clearly. This is the result of the ear's design, a model that has evolved to work best in air. The hydrophone provides a wonderful interface enabling us to detect organisms that vocalize there.

If you happen to be in the right marine environment where a particular whale sound is loud enough and your boat is single-hulled, you may be able to detect the sounds of humpbacks, bowheads, and killer whales through the hull. Sailors and Eskimo hunters have often reported hearing these animal vocalizations in just such a manner. In certain forests, some creatures prefer to vocalize at night, when dew settles on the ground or on the leaves and branches of trees. Using the forest as a reverberant theater, or a kind of echo chamber, nighttime becomes their time to "sing." Particular nocturnal birds, hyenas, baboons, coyotes, and wolves often choose reverberant environments, or special times when the conditions in the environment produce reverberation, in which to vocalize. They even change their voices slightly to accommodate for the echo. Bull elk rutting in the fall often use the echoes of the forest to project their voices in order to extend their territory and secure harems. Killer and humpback whales sometimes vocalize in air, bouncing their voices off nearby cliffs along the shores of Glacier Bay, Alaska, and other environs, such as Johnstone Strait off the eastern shore of Vancouver Island in Canada. While camping on Point Adolphus along the northern shore of Chichagof Island, just west of Juneau, my wife and I heard several members of a humpback pod virtually trumpet twenty yards away from where we slept. They chose that spot to rest after long hours of daytime feeding. Some insects, birds, and mammals like to vocalize when the habitat dries out—after sunrise when the forest has given up its surface moisture and animal voices don't need to carry so far, while others prefer transition periods neither dry nor reverberant.

Once you've found your quiet spot, listen (preferably with eyes closed) to the ways in which the combinations of creature voices define the space. The biophony will appear to change as you move from place to place through the landscape and as day and night, seasons and weather shift through their cycles. The territories defined by the biophonies can be quite small and shaped differently from what you might expect. Each type of habitat even within the same biome will provide a number of unique biophonic experiences as distinctive as our individual voices. The natural world above and even below the ground, above and below the surface of water, is everywhere alive with vibration.

The fish does . . . HIP
The bird does . . . VISS

The marmot does . . . GNAN
I throw myself to the left,
I turn myself to the right,
I act the fish,
Which darts in the water, which darts
Which twists about, which leaps—
All lives, all dances, and all is loud.
—*Gabon Pygmy, Africa, from* Technicians of the Sacred

I've often heard that the vocal amplitude (loudness) of a creature depends on its size. In other words, small creatures have tiny, soft voices, and larger animals are always louder. Careful listening will dispel this myth. Many small creatures have voices so loud that, if extrapolated pound for pound into larger beasts and heard, every living organism within hearing range would become instantly deaf. Consider the snapping shrimp, a crustacean only an inch and a half (3.8 cm) long. The popping sound it produces underwater is equivalent to the impact noise in air of a .357 magnum pistol being shot off near your ear. Imagine a snapping shrimp the size of an elephant with a correspondingly loud voice. Other small and very loud creatures that immediately come to mind are the Pacific tree frog (about the size of your little fingernail), whose voice registers about 80 dBA at ten feet (three meters). Rock or tree hyraxes and the mynah bird are other examples of loud small creatures. On the other hand, many large creatures have relatively soft voices, like the giraffe (except for its low-frequency sounds), the California gray whale, tapirs, and anteaters.

To hear this range of sounds, try different ways to listen. Cup your hands behind your ears and slowly turn around. Notice how sounds become louder and more focused. You'll hear more because the surface of your ears that collects sound just got bigger.[4] You'll begin to hear as some animals with large ears do and understand how the shapes and sizes of their ears help creatures locate the direction a sound comes from. Cut some paper into patterns shaped like the ears of other mammals (or print them using a 3D printer). Model them so that they can be taped to your own ears or on the stems of eyeglasses. This will give you an idea about the ways in which other creatures might hear and how listening might be refocused and enhanced.

Listen with your eyes closed or blindfolded. Walk toward a stream. See if you can determine how far you are from the water's edge by sound alone. Still blindfolded, face in the direction of a singing bird. Try to tell how near or far away it might be, or, if it moves to another tree, in what direction it has flown. Just be aware that some birds can fool you by singing or calling in a way that makes you think their voice is coming from a direction other than where it's actually located.

Questions to consider as you move through these exercises:

- How many different types or families of animal sounds do you hear?
- Within each group of sounds, how many different species can you identify?
- Are you able to distinguish between one site and another just by the subtle difference in biophonies?
- How would you describe the acoustic textures you hear? (Expand on the usual descriptions like *buzz, coo, tweet, whoop, peep, cluck, cackle, hum, hoot, shriek, hiss, gurgle, pulsate, moan, groan, belch, chatter, whisper, rhythmic, scratch, ringing, bellow, pant, breathy, reverberant,* and *dry sounding.*)

Don't limit yourself to the larger species, those you can easily see. The very small creatures, nearly microscopic, sing too, and have wonderful sound signatures. Several species of ants, insect larvae in pools of water, water boatmen, anemones, and fish all generate recognizable and unique sounds. Earthworms create sound signatures as they travel through the soil. Even viruses create sound signatures particular to each type.[5] Generally, it's the smaller creature voices that have given me the most amusement because they are so surprising. Many species of bats, insects, and numerous marine organisms require specialized (but not too expensive) equipment to enable you to hear them. And some bioacousticians now believe that every living organism produces an acoustic signature. So you've got a lifetime of exploration to do.

When recording or listening critically, I generally prefer to be alone. Even my own presence introduces a certain amount of noise and distraction to the Others (as the late Paul Shepard referred to non-human organisms). My stomach grumbles, or I hear myself trying to brush away or slap at annoying insects. Listening in groups can only be done if everyone is dedicated to being very still and quiet. No talking. No rustling of clothing. No shuffling of feet, coughing, clearing of throats, or sniffling. You don't have to hold your breath. Just be cool and considerate. Leave all other thoughts behind and concentrate entirely on what you're hearing and recording.

From the outset, with newly trained ears, try to grasp the aural context in which these creatures vocalize. Focus on all the sounds that make up the entire animal orchestra. Notice how they blend and the sources from which they come. Along with those, be particularly mindful of the subtle differences in acoustic flow of streams, creeks, waterfalls, and sand dunes singing, cells of thunder and rain passing through, wind in the aspens, pines, or maples, wave action at the shore; listen to the proto-orchestration conveyed by whole environments.

Most of us hear the sound of crickets, katydids, or other insects and frogs as a cacophony or din of noise. In modern society, this is symptomatic of how we emphasized our sense of sight over other senses. When you listen closely, you begin to discern a wealth of information from sound-producing organisms. For instance, did you know that you can determine the temperature in air by counting the number of chirps made by certain crickets? In the evening, listen to the rhythms they produce. Crickets do this by rubbing their wings together. One wing has a *scraper,* the other a *file.* Sound occurs when the wing containing the scraper rubs against the wing with the file. The friction between these two body parts is called stridulation. Because crickets are cold-blooded, the tempo of the stridulation, or number of pulses in a given period of time, is based on the ambient temperature and its effect on the temperature of their bodies. Count the chirp pulses the snowy tree cricket (*Oecantus fultoni*) produces in fifteen seconds, add forty to it, and you'll find the temperature at its location in Fahrenheit. Other species have different formulae that are similarly easy to determine (you can add the number of pulses that occur in fifteen seconds to a prescribed number depending on the species). By reversing the equation you can determine what the formula is for each particular species of cricket in your own backyard or on the trail. Sometimes, during evenings that have cooled quickly, following a very hot day, the crickets within your range of hearing do not have a synchronous stridulation. The ground temperature varies because some areas have been exposed to the sun while others have been in the shade. So some crickets will chirp at a slower rate where the ground is cooler while other groups are chirping at a faster rate where the ground is warmer. Sooner or later, during the course of the evening, the temperatures will equalize and all the chirping pulses will be expressed at more or less the same rate. You can also set up an inexpensive exhibit in your house that features the temperature-revealing knack of crickets. All you need is a cricket in a glass jar with an open top, a hidden but accessible thermometer, and a chart with the formula printed on it. Using the sounds of the cricket chirps and the following formula, what is the temperature here?

I borrow an allusion from crickets:
"their song is useless,
it serves no purpose
this sonorous scraping of wings
But without the indecipherable signal
transmitted from one to another
the night would not
(to crickets)
    be night."
—*José Emilio Pacheco, "Defense and Illustration of Poetry"*

Compare related habitats. Now that you've had a chance to listen in one spot, move anywhere from fifty to a few hundred feet away and listen to what the soundscape tells you from your new location. Notice how the sounds of the insects have subtly changed. Perhaps it's the mix of birds and insects occupying this new territory because the properties of the vegetation or the contours of the landscape have changed, or because you moved closer to a pond, you now hear bullfrogs. Explore its acoustic boundaries to get a sense of the territory's shape as it is defined by sound. The flora and geological features may look the same, but check for subtle acoustic differences. As you cross from one zone to another, the creature mix defines the territory with even greater precision than what you can experience visually. This may be a result of the territorial syntax (slight changes in the phrasing arrangement as expressed in the soundscape because of the acoustic properties of the habitat's landscape and geological features). Don't think of these territorial shapes as geometric squares or circles with sides or diameters measuring a hundred yards each. In the natural world, the acoustic boundaries of biomes tend to be more fluid and often shift their borders as they fluctuate over the course of each day, night, or season. Where allowed, legal, safe, and encouraged, don't be afraid to leave the formal trail to discover how a territory is conveyed through the vocalizations of the constituent biophonic chorus. Watch out for poison oak or ivy and the occasional snake, though. And always check for ticks.

After you've tried this exercise out in the wild, review what you've heard and think about how all of the sounds fit together or interact, or conversely, how they do not. When the vocalizations you hear seem not to relate, these dissonances or conflicts may be a result of an environment's alteration or stress. After a forest has been clear-cut, for example, or even when it has been thinned and shows signs of regeneration, it takes some time before vocal creatures reestablish their niches so they can be heard in concert once again.

Tips for Field Trips

- Never leave home without taking a few pencils or pens and a notebook with you into the field. (Leave iPad, smartphones, and laptop behind. A pencil never runs out of battery power.)
- Write down everything you hear in as much detail as you can.
- Draw maps (even crude ones) of the territories that distinguish one soundscape within a territory from another. If you have a GPS

device, make a note of the GPS coordinates so that you can revisit your favorite locations in the future. Your smartphone likely has this capability (and several apps that feature the ability to note the waypoint of your latitude and longitude).

• Describe the sounds you detect and characterize their differing effects on you. A particular soundscape in the vicinity of the Tetons may include birds like the mountain chickadee, Wilson's warbler, warbling vireo, yellow warbler, white-crowned sparrow, house wren, dusky flycatcher, and hairy woodpecker, or the chattering of a ground squirrel. It may also include a stream in the background or the effect of wind blowing through the trees (try to find the vocabulary or phrase clear enough to make distinctions between the noise of the stream, wind effect, and rain, especially since these geophonies share characteristics of white noise). The soundscape may also include the drips of water on leaves after a rainstorm has passed, the silence after a snowstorm or in a desert box canyon, something your eye didn't catch skittering through a pile of leaves on the ground, the particular way a forest resonates after a night of rain and the way it soaks up and attenuates reverberation after the sun rises and dries things out.

> In the clearing, where the mind flowers
> and the world sprouts up at every side,
> listen
> for the sound in the bushes
> behind the grass.
> —*Marcia Falk, "Listen"*

4

The Language of Soundscapes:
New Words for Old Sounds

Songs are thoughts, sung out with the breath when people are
moved by great forces and ordinary speech no longer suffices . . .
it will happen that the words we need will come of themselves.
When the words we want to use shoot up of themselves—we get
a new song.

— *Statement by Orpingalik, a Netsilik Eskimo, from*
Technicians of the Sacred

Our spoken language contains few references to sound in the
natural world. While our speech is full of visual descriptions or words
that define the physical characteristics of objects we see, it is short
on vocabulary to describe what we hear. Even our musical lexicon is
replete with terms for sound based on the language of sight, such as
color, form, dark, or *light.* My experience in scoring films showed me
that almost all of the expressions used to talk about film music and
composition are laced with visual phrases. Since there are few words
to describe the music needed to enhance a scene, directors would frequently say things like, 'Try *shaping* the scene this way,' 'I'm looking
for this kind of *color* in the orchestration.' 'Can you make the orchestration *brighter?*' 'Can you make it *darker?*' And, 'I'm looking for a

softer *texture*.' Very few directors could conceptualize what they wished to hear in aural, musical, or any other acoustic terms, even when they were musically trained themselves.

At many points along this journey, I was looking for a word to describe the combined and related sound that creatures make in a particular location, and I turned to Latin or Greek roots that would easily define a character of natural sound. *Animal symphony* or *orchestra* was way too cumbersome. The *niche hypothesis* was still too complicated. My collaboration with Stuart Gage inspired the ideas of geophony and anthropophony as sources of sound, fleshing out and putting words to what I was hearing, and rounding out the original animal-voice concept, biophony, that I had identified earlier. Even so, we still have much work to do to expand our vocabulary enough so that it fully describes the subtleties of non-creature, non-human acoustic signatures in an environment—the sounds of water, wind blowing through different types of trees, thunder and rain, and the vibrant world of the Others. Once, when I heard sand dunes singing and I didn't have a word to describe the source, I longed for a simple expression for it. So when Gage proposed the term *geophony* to add to my concept of biophony, a whole new world of possibilities opened up, and singing dunes fit right in. We need much more descriptive material about sonic experiences and welcome anything you have to offer.

Here's a typical problem: crickets "chirp." Well, so do birds. We need to find more precise words to help distinguish the sounds. For one thing, the sound-producing mechanism in birds, a syrinx, is different from that of a cricket scraping its wings together. Crickets and other insects produce incredible varieties of sounds. Many crickets produce a pitched sound that is both pulsed and rhythmic. Crickets can also produce sound by moving their wings in different ways—sometimes referred to as a *chirr*—a rapid series of amplitude-modulated (loud to soft) tones. A bird's song or call, on the other hand, can be many times more complex, with several tones and overtones articulated at the same time. In our descriptive language, however, a chirp—whether from bird, insect, or mammal—remains a chirp.

In English, the contented sound of our domestic cat, Barnacle, is called a *purr*. This conveys nothing about the character of the cat's voice that reaches my ear. The French word, *ronron,* especially when expressed with the French "r," comes a lot closer to the sound of the otherwise contented cats I know and love. However, there is still only one way to articulate the cat's voice of tranquility. Birders have their own mysterious lexicon. An American robin is described in one book as vocalizing, *cheer-up, cheerily, cheer-up, cheerily.* Right! Turn that around and have someone read that to you and try to guess what bird they're trying to describe. As we pay more attention to the substance of these voices, and devote some imagination to expanding the language, we will be more able to improve our biophonic descriptions.

As simple field recording gear became more accessible in the past few years, listeners and recordists were becoming more mindful of the gap between what they experienced in the acoustic world and what they found themselves able to describe. Yet in our attempt to characterize voices in the wild we often resort to esoteric musical terms, since music is where our attention to sound has generally been focused. From the latter half of the fifteenth century, a variety of musical expressions—most developed in Italy—became common in the language of classical composition. From time to time I fall back on these terms to describe elements of sound. The accompanying table lists examples of these musical terms, along with their original definitions as well as an example of how they have been extended to bioacoustic field work.

Musical term	Original definition	Bioacoustic definition
Accelerando	It. Getting faster	Accelerating sounds, as with the wingbeats of a ruffed grouse.
Accent	L. Stressing a particular note or beat.	Common in the calls and songs of many birds, frogs, and insects, or in drumming of the great apes on the buttresses of fig trees in their respective forests.
Aeolian	Gr. Sound produced by wind.	Wind blowing through barbed wire, snags of wood, reeds by a stream broken at different lengths, or the needles of pine trees and the leaves of aspens. A whistle-like tone that rises or lowers in pitch depending on the force of the gusts and the medium affected.
Allegro	It. Cheerful or a fast tempo.	On the cheery side—such as birdsong on a spring morning.
Andante	It. Literally means to walk.	I usually think of this as an insect or frog rhythm, moderately paced, which intuitively inspires body movement, as we were once impelled to do in ancient times.
Appoggiatura	It. Refers to certain notes of a melody moving quickly from one to another either above or below a commonly produced tone.	Frogs and birds sometimes embellish their vocalizations in this manner, as do some species of whales and dolphins.

Musical term	Original definition	Bioacoustic definition
Arpeggio	*It.* The single notes of a chord played in rapid succession, either up or down in pitch, articulated like those played on a harp.	Heard in some humpback whale song recordings. Also, the song of a Swainson's thrush.
Bagatelle	*It.* The term first appeared in the early 19th century to denote a short character piece.	In Amazonia, you'll find this type of articulation in the voices of the common potoo and the musician wren. Another, the screaming piha, whistles the fifth note in the Western scale, followed by the tonic or main note, then moves up a fourth and begins the whole sequence all over again in another key.
Drone or pedal-point	A constant tone or sound over which all other voices make themselves heard in particular.	The collective ongoing sound of insects in a rainforest at certain times of day or night. Often experienced in the wild in many forms.
Duet	*It.* A performance in two parts.	Often heard among birds, whales, frogs, and gibbons.
Dynamism	Characterized by loud and soft, percussive and non-percussive. Lately noted in Western culture as a kind of musical expression early in the 20th century with composers like Stravinsky.	An expression of nearly all biomes, marine and terrestrial, that has always been present in the natural world.

(continued)

Musical term	Original definition	Bioacoustic definition
Ear training	Learning to make distinctions between one tone and another, between the sounds of one instrument and another.	Becoming familiar again with the sounds that make up biophonies in different environments. Learning to listen.
Falsetto	*It.* Singing above one's normal range; thought in academia to be an ability unique to humans.	Lots of non-human creatures use this technique when singing: humpback whales, for instance, or my cat.
Fermata	*It.* Pause.	As you approach a pond full of croaking bullfrogs, note what happens.
Flauto	*It.* Flute-like.	The best example is the song of the *flautista* or musician wren.
Frog	The hand grip for a violin, cello, or string bass bow.	As Ambrose Bierce suggests: "A creature with edible legs."
Glissando	*It.* A rapid, smooth slide from one pitch to another.	Many birds, whales, and land-based mammals produce vocalizations that exhibit this characteristic. Sand dunes singing are non-creature examples.
Gong	*Malay.* A round orchestral percussion instrument usually made of brass and struck with a mallet to produce a deep and complex bell-like sound.	The metallic sound produced biologically by the walrus.
Harmonic	*L. & Gr.* The relationship of one tone or voice to another. Also, the complex series of measurable tones within a single note.	Vocal organisms, in order to establish unimpeded bandwidth so that their signals are not masked, find clear niches within the harmonic structure of the audio spectrum.

Musical term	Original definition	Bioacoustic definition
Improvisation (*jam*)	*Jam* is the American jazz term for improvisation.	Since creatures taught us to dance and sing, they also taught us to jam long before Louis Armstrong appeared on the scene. Bayaka pygmies and Tuva singers demonstrate their ability to improvise with the voices of their natural surroundings in complex ways we can only aspire to.
Legato	*It.* A smooth transition from tone to tone.	Sometimes found in whales, land mammals, and birdsong along with biophonic transitions from dawn to daytime and dusk to evening.
Meter	*L. & Fr.* Beats or accents defining time.	The natural world expresses itself in broad cycles of day/night or seasons. Frogs and crickets establish pulses of time, or lyrical rhythms usually heard at night. Cicadas begin their buzzing definitions of time when the sun momentarily penetrates the canopies of rainforests throughout the world. Chimps and other forest-dwelling primates pound out distinctive rhythms on the buttresses of fig (ficus) trees.
Ostinato	*It.* A persistently repeated phrase. In jazz, it is called a *riff*.	The song of a robin in spring.

(*continued*)

Musical term	Original definition	Bioacoustic definition
Poco adagio	*It.* Kind of slow.	The rate at which we as a civilization are moving toward ecological sanity.
Polyphony	*Gr.* Many voices, according to most musical history books. It first appeared in the lexicon in the 9th century. It has been a part of non-Western music for at least 30,000 years, according to some anthropologists.	Non-human creatures have been expressing themselves in this form for perhaps 60 million years. A common feature of biophony.
Polyrhythm	*Gr.* Many rhythms expressed at the same time.	A common feature of biophony.
Presto	*It.* Quick!	The rate at which you'll jump when spotting a rattlesnake. Similar to the rate at which natural soundscape is disappearing.
Rhythm	*Gr.* Regular recurrence of strong and weak beats.	For millions of years, chimps have been pounding out rhythms in the forests of Africa. Crickets and frogs have been dividing the time of night with their wide variety of voices. As I write this, there is a piliated woodpecker outside my window punctuating the moment with percussive hits on the trunk of a hollowed-out tree.

Musical term	Original definition	Bioacoustic definition
Scat	American term referring to a form of jazz singing made popular by Cab Calloway.	Thrushes commonly express themselves this way. So does the siamang (a type of gibbon) and baby mountain gorilla. Probably some whales too. *Then* came humans.
Timbre	*Fr.* The particular quality of a voice, sometimes referred to as color.	In the natural world, it is the unique quality of each individual voice, but also the type of organic soundscape produced in a biome; the aural texture of its biophony.

Aside from words like *loud, soft, explosive,* and others common in the language, most of us quickly reach our limitations with the available vocabulary. In his book *Spell of the Sensuous,* David Abram challenges us to come up with new words to describe aspects of the natural wild. Abram's work is based in large part on the writings of Maurice Merleau-Ponty, a French philosopher, who wrote that language "is the very voice of the trees, the waves, and the forests."[1]

Because of a renewed interest in sounds of the natural world, however, there are positive signs that our slim descriptive vocabulary may be changing. Professional listeners, like composers, poets, and field recordists, have been foremost in this search for new language. Joachim-Ernst Berendt, in his book *The Third Ear,* relates a moment he experienced at a lake in Oregon's Cascade Mountains one summer's day.

I am lying on a bed of pine needles by the water . . . Closer at hand, flies flitting past, dragonflies dancing, mosquitoes circling. Not much for the eyes.

But I hear: silence. It is the silence which I hear first of all. Like a weight that I can grasp. A heavy, smooth weight. My ears feel it as if they were groping fingers. I observe that the weight feels good. I think: You haven't heard such silence for a long time.

I occupy myself with: silence. It is alive. A drop of silence. My ears penetrate it. I am inside it. The drop becomes a universe. A cosmos that begins to resound.

This is the cosmos. First of all, the lake. A rhythmic gurgling. A deep sound—bubbling somewhat—and two higher notes: splashing and sploshing. Triple time, as if the lake were dancing a waltz. This isn't a joyous dance. Rather listless, self-forgetful, leisurely . . .

The deep gurgling sounds like a tired tom-tom. The two higher notes are wooden, like a ballophone, the West African xylophone. A lake playing tom-tom and ballophone.

Then the first dragonfly makes itself felt. I hear it before I can actually see it. The whirring of its rotating wings. The primordial helicopter. Still more functional than any made by man. More dragonflies follow and I discover: there are many different dragonfly sounds. Higher notes, whirrings fast and slow, and dark dronings. And all possible gradations in between. A scale performed by dragonflies. It is long before I am aware that it is only seldom that a dragonfly comes buzzing by.

. . . But then—even outdoing those voices—a mosquito like a muted trumpet. Like Miles Davis. Piercing. Striking. A flash of lightning for the ear.

The lower the sun sinks, the more sumptuous the concert becomes. From double-bassoon to piccolo, each instrument glissandos into the next. Duos, trios, quartets, chamber ensembles. . . . The water's rhythmic pattern expands. Now I can count up to five before it repeats itself. The gurgling incoming swell approaches to a count of three and recedes to a count of two: a quintuple rhythm not to be found in music. The stress is exactly in the middle: on the third beat. In music five beats to the bar usually involve triple and duple time—or the other way around. First comes the duple and then the triple time. The water 'Five in a bar' of my lake in Oregon consists of two duple times separated by a sombre thud in between. No resemblance to 'Take Five' by Dave Brubeck and Paul Desmond, the piece which helped so many people [in the West] learn to hear 'Fives.'

Not every professional listener, like Berendt, has been as concerned with translating natural sound into spoken language. During walks in the woods with his wife, Yvonne, Olivier Messiaen, the mid-twentieth-century avant-garde French composer, would note in some detail the birdsongs he found especially melodic, and incorporate variations into his compositions. Although Messiaen was a fine naturalist and devoted birder, he almost never gave the calls or songs terms of expression in his native language. Perhaps he felt the language of music was more precise in its ability to re-create creature expressions in the natural world. While he attempted to represent some individual creature sounds, he never produced a full vocabulary or musical representation of either the birds he noted or the more complex biophonies he engaged with. How do you capture and replicate the roar of a lion, the stridulation of an ant, the complexities of the song of a Swainson's thrush, a parrot fish, a long-horned sculpin (fish), or the sound signature of earthworms penetrating their soil-bound worlds? Likewise, the soundscape of a lake habitat with its mixture of insects, frogs, and loons, all at once with common musical notation or non-electronic orchestral instruments? We all know that ravens "call," with a huge vocabulary that is quite remarkable. Except for the word *call* itself, our language lacks terms for the vast range of their vocalizations.

Composers tend to deconstruct and fragment the natural world just as scientists have been doing. Where science adheres to study models they can replicate, composers likewise incline toward emulating those sounds that fit the musical paradigms of their respective cultures. Most are apt to leave out sounds they cannot reproduce in musical notation or define verbally. As experimental artists, John Cage and Messiaen nevertheless failed to include the sound of a crocodile, a hippo, a wildebeest, or a spadefoot toad (or any toad) in their compositions. What did they find attractive about some voices and not useful about others? Well, Cage and Messiaen weren't alone. Most of Western nature-inspired musical literature is defined by its woefully limited fascination with key emblematic creatures: a few whales, wolves, and less than a hundred of the ten thousand species of birds that exist. Until very recently, the reason that most composers favored some sounds and not others largely reflected the cultural biases by which they have decided that certain creature expressions are beautiful, significant and musical, while most of the others are not.

R. Murray Schafer, on the other hand, is a fine contemporary example of our nexus to and harmony between the natural world and music. Examples of his work are featured on a recording titled *Once on a Windy Night.*[2] In the title piece, Schafer uses the sound produced by wind—arguably the most difficult natural sound to replicate— and generates a choral piece that is both breathtaking (pardon the pun) and potent. Because we're visually oriented, it seems easier for us to describe elements of a landscape in terms of what they look like (types of trees or vegetation; flat or hilly terrain; green, brown, light, dark, sunny or foggy; animals, no animals, humans, no humans, urban, rural, and so on). These descriptions have become rather commonplace in our visual vocabulary and we almost take them for granted. Schafer's work has triggered new interest in that mode of enquiry.

When I ask people to describe their favorite natural sound, they invariably choose between two broad types: either marine or ter-restrial. Using no particular words to describe them, they usually mention ocean waves, a stream, waterfalls, or rain, on one hand, or forests, birds in spring, deserts, or mountains on the other. The dy-namic of natural soundscapes runs the gamut from the softest to the loudest sounds heard on the planet, and includes the lowest to high-est frequency sounds in the realm of creature life. The power of this range contains a force that is infectious and, at the same time, subtle and animated. Within the range of sounds we hear is a miraculous abundance of information. The problem is that most of this spec-tacular data is ignored or remains unprocessed with no cipher yet to transform and support it.

As I mentioned earlier, sound-wise I was educated to deconstruct whole, healthy systems into their intrinsic parts, from the dissection of frogs and small domestic organisms to analysis of creature voices that were split from their original contexts. Generally the subject voices were presented piece by piece for consideration. No vocabu-lary expressed the holistic manner in which these organisms existed.

My first courses in bioacoustics in the late 1960s were no different. Bird vocalizations were broken down into species' calls or songs, the limit of their expression. Coyotes or wolves either yipped, barked, or howled. Dolphins clicked or screamed. Humpbacks sang or uttered contact vocalizations.

Every living creature has a sound signature—from the smallest microorganism to the largest megafauna. Even some vegetation! Long ago, I was sent to record corn growing in Iowa. Over a couple of hot August evenings, I sat in a remote field with my recorder and mics, swarmed by mosquitoes and fighting off flies. Around midnight, I heard an increasing volume of popping sounds as the stalks of corn began their evening expansion, telescoping in length almost perceptibly in the moonlight, the friction between tightly wrapped layers causing them to squeak and pop, hence the sound signature of corn growing. My Iowa exile that summer led to a moment of pure pleasure; every sound connected in a vibrant interrelationship magnified by the use of my recording gear. I'm still trying to find words to describe the voice of growing corn.

5

The Art of Hearing and Recording

God asks nothing of the highest soul but attention.

—*Henry David Thoreau*

Although we can hear a large number of natural sounds with our ears alone, to hear others we need some help. Just as it is impossible to see certain organisms without the aid of a magnifying glass, microscope, or binoculars, some voices likewise need assistance to be heard. These small sounds are really exciting to explore. I never could have heard the sounds of the anemones in Alaska, for instance, without the aid of a hydrophone, an amplifier and recorder, and a pair of headphones.

Check out the acoustic signatures of whales and ants, and you'll come to know, first hand, just how useful sound-capture technologies—microphones, hydrophones, and recorders—can be.

A Brief History of Sound Recording

The recording of natural sounds began in 1889, when Ludwig Koch, then only eight years old, recorded a white-rumped shama (*Copyschus malabaricus*) on an Edison wax cylinder recorder in his backyard. At that moment, the foundation was laid for the field of soundscape ecology. It took nearly a century, however, before this discipline became even partially recognized in academia. While some European countries, like Italy and France, have advanced bioacoustic curricula, as of this writing in the United States the field is difficult to find in all but a minimal number of undergraduate and graduate environmental studies programs.

Soon after Edison's wax cylinder was commercialized and became a popular success, Valdemar Poulsen, a Danish scientist, invented his Telegraphone, or wire recorder, in 1898. The first electronically driven system used to record sound, the recording medium consisted of a thin wire fed at a constant rate from one reel to another past an electronically magnetized recording head. Poulsen's invention paved the way for storage, manipulation, and retrieval of large, more minutely detailed samples of recorded information. One of the main problems with this technology was that the wires the signal was recorded on often became crimped or knotted, greatly affecting the cohesion of the sound. In addition, the wire tended to become unraveled when not under constant tension. Still, rudimentary audio editing became possible for the first time; all it required was cutting the wire and tying the ends together, although this soon proved impractical.

Around the same time, various forms of flat disk recording systems were patented by Edison, RCA, and other companies. These readily available consumer products quickly became popular for recording and storing sound. It wasn't until the late 1920s, however, following AT&T's invention of the Vitaphone, that a method of capturing and reproducing sound on film—referred to in the industry as *optical sound tracks*—made possible the reproduction of natural sound, and initiating a conscious effort to do so. Warner Brothers acquired the rights to the Vitaphone process and approached the Cornell Department of Ornithology, offering to work with the department to record the sounds of birds on film. The company's engineers would demonstrate the technical excellence of their invention, and Cornell's bird specialists would identify the creatures and allow Warner Brothers to use the recordings in their film sound tracks.

At the heart of optical sound technology is the use of light. In this case it consisted of tiny narrow strips of alternating black and clear images, resembling tiny bar codes, that ran the length of one side of the film strip, synching the sound to the picture. This representation of sound, read by a beam of light cast through the striated patterns, projected the variations onto a photoelectric cell in order to create pulses of sound. The first Cornell field recording team of Arthur Allen, Albert Brand, and Peter Paul Kellogg was formed in the spring of 1935. Brand brought with him a piece of equipment referred to as a *sound mirror*—actually the forerunner of the parabolic dish—a device used to capture sound a considerable distance from the microphone. The bulky, complex, and heavy equipment was loaded onto the back of an old mule-drawn wagon and dragged through marshes in the southeastern United States to a remote location. There, they captured a recording of the nearly extinct ivory-billed woodpecker—its demise still disputed.

When a German group invented the Magnetaphone in the late 1930s, the possibilities of recording extended samples in the field became even more feasible. The engineers who invented this medium used long, thin, quarter-inch strips of paper tape coated with fine particles of iron oxide, which, like its wire-dependent predecessor, was drawn at a constant speed across an electromagnetic head, the surface of which was a bit smaller than a human thumbnail. The head delivered a variable magnetic impulse representing an analog of sound that rearranged the particles of oxide into patterns symbolizing the speech or music captured at the input of the system. Once recorded on tape, it could then be easily rewound, played back, and edited. The Germans used it as a surveillance device and for propaganda during World War II, broadcasting Hitler's speeches from different locations at different times, confusing the Allied communications experts. During the postwar occupation of Europe, the Ampex Corporation, from Palo Alto, California, acquired the technology, and its engineers improved both the frequency response and dynamic quality of the audiotape by tweaking the recording electronics and obtained several patents on the process in 1948. With that in hand they created a type of reel-to-reel system that endured for more than fifty years, and is still used to record some music sessions even today.

Between Edison's day and the late 1960s—with the exception of researchers associated with Cornell, a few marine biologists connected with the Navy's submarine warfare program, and a handful of recordists professionally involved in film sound design—very few people were interested in, or committed to, the recording of natural soundscapes. Most naturalists and biologists chose instead to capture the essence of the natural world with pictorial images on film or canvas, and paid almost no attention to the principal thrust of communication by animals, their unique sound signatures. Those few who were devoted to sound recording put their main effort into the isolation of single creature voices, separating them out from the surrounding aural context. This became the standard academic model, and in many quarters it remains so today. Researchers tended to overlook the sounds of whole habitats, considering them insignificant or too complex to fully grasp.

Outside of academia, the magnitude of natural soundscape's significance wasn't considered seriously, either. In fact, it was so overlooked that as recently as the late 1970s, the call of the Australian kookaburra bird could still be heard inserted into the sound effect tracks of both popular and nature films that were obviously shot on locations in the Amazon, Costa Rica, or the Everglades. Pictures of bald eagles in flight would often be accompanied by the screams of a red-tailed hawk. Media producers cynically justified these choices by asserting that the general public wouldn't know the difference or care. To a certain point they were absolutely right. To most of the public, the call of the kookaburra, heard in the early Tarzan and Jane movies made in the 1930s and 1940s, came to symbolize the acoustic signature of "the jungle." According to those I have talked with from that era, it was not the job of the movie director to either educate or disappoint people.

There was one exception to the ignorance of natural sound that not only startled many in the last century, but also brought attention to a field that was previously unknown. When the first recordings of humpback whales were released in 1968, the overwhelming public response caught record executives completely off guard. These humpback whale "songs," recorded by researchers Roger and Katy Payne, were the first marine examples most people had ever heard.[1] The wondrous variety of musical-like themes emanating from a world other than their own captivated listeners. The magic of these recordings caught my attention and drew me to explore wild soundscapes in more detail. It also captured the creative imaginations of serious composers and popular artists like George Crumb, Alan Hovhaness, Paul Winter, and Judy Collins. Technology had also progressed enough that amateur and semiprofessional listening and recording equipment became both affordable and easy to use. Natural sound's effect on us is powerful. This is particularly true of stereo field recordings. If they're recorded right, these two-channel correlated audio programs can generate numinous illusions every time they are played back. When they're at their best, nothing in the human-created visual world, by itself, even comes close to their impact. Before describing some of the simpler recording technologies, it's important to understand how we hear.

Our ears receive vibrations that move through the air with a great enough amplitude that we can hear them and within a range of frequencies we can detect. For those of us blessed with good hearing, our brains process the incoming signals so we can discriminate between bits of desired information and those that are not. And by subtle changes in phase and Doppler shift, we are also able to determine which direction sound is coming from in all planes—up or down, from left to right across the spectrum, or front to back.

The physical shape of the *pinna,* or outer ear, helps us to collect and amplify sound waves. The pinna collects the signals and channels them into the external auditory canal, where the acoustic waves are modified—becoming subtly different from what originally arrived at the outer ear (figure 8). As the sound travels through the auditory canal, it is greatly amplified because of its shape—sometimes by a factor of two (particularly in the 2–4 kHz range). Because the ear is particularly sensitive in this region of the audio spectrum, loud noises in this frequency range can be particularly hazardous to our hearing.

The external auditory canal ends at the *tympanic* membrane, which most refer to as the eardrum. This membrane protects the middle ear from foreign bodies, and it also vibrates in response to the small changes in air pressure, transmitting those vibrations into the middle ear. There, a series of three small bones, commonly called the hammer (*malleus*), anvil (*incus*), and stirrup (*stapes*), connect to the oval or round window of the inner ear, the semicircular canals, which in turn lead to a fluid-filled cavity consisting of the cochlea.

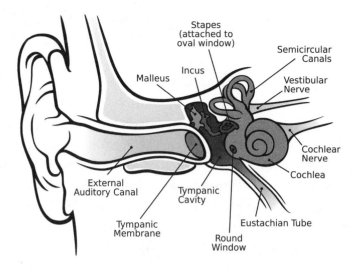

8. "Anatomy of the Human Ear" (from "Perception Space—The Final Frontier," by Lars Chittka and Axel Brockmann, *PLoS Biology* 3 (2005), no. 4: e137; doi:10.1371/journal.pbio.0030137, fig. 1A/large version, copyright 2005 by Chittka and Brockmann, vectorised by Inductiveload, licensed under Creative Commons Attribution 2.5 via Wikimedia Commons)

With mammals the length of the cochlea helps determine the frequency range that we are able to hear. Numerous tiny hair cells in the cochlea are set into motion by the vibrations that have managed to reach the inner ear. Finally, the signals that have survived the journey through the outer, middle, and inner ear reach the auditory nerve, then travel to the acoustic processing centers of the brain, which analyze the signals, helping us to separate "noise" from useful information.[2]

Much of the sound that reaches our ears is unwanted information, or noise, such as traffic, loud din in a restaurant when we want to hear what our companion is saying, background clatter in offices with large open spaces, industrial racket (either indoors or out), and various types of aircraft. For those of us who dwell in urban environments, our brains have adapted to noise and learned how to filter out many of these sounds, while simultaneously retaining and processing what we consider essential. Nevertheless, the noise exists and our brains do a lot of work trying to mask it for us.

In some vocations, like those of professional musicians, discriminating listening becomes a major feature of everyday life. Even there, what many musicians learn to listen to and for is often limited to the structure of certain types of compositions and the roles their instruments play in replicating those models. The best musicians hear a much broader range of sounds than those of us with untrained ears. Listening to the voices of the natural world requires similar levels of hearing discrimination. The layers and textures of sound can extend from simple to very complex—just like orchestral compositions. The difference with natural soundscapes is that they can be many times more expressive, intricate, and expansive than the most elegant symphonic music.

The human ear, bound by physiological and neural restrictions, has a limited ability to hear very low (infrasound) and very high (ultrasound) signals. It is also restricted by its capacities to hear signals that are extremely soft in volume or very loud, which can cause damage or even deafness. However, our ears are especially sensitive to spatial discrimination. We can differentiate sound coming from overhead, to the right or left of us, in back, and up and down. We can also recognize the difference between voices. Some ornithologists with well-honed listening skills can distinguish the subtle differences between local and regional dialects in birds of the same species. The ear is a wonderfully dynamic tool; there is no known technology that replaces its performance characteristics. However, some of the newer technologies are pretty effective at replicating a few of them.

Getting Started with Simple Sound Recording Equipment

With contemporary equipment, recording sound is as easy as taking a photograph with your smartphone. In fact, you can actually record pretty successfully with a smartphone (with any of several mic attachments). But when I want to capture some memorable reminder of my journey, I travel with a dedicated recorder. With recordings, I highlight my journeys in ways unthinkable with just a camera. I play the soundscapes for anyone who will listen. I use them to evoke memories of the trip, or, in some cases, produce an audio product like an album download or a performance piece like a symphony, ballet, or an installation in a public museum or visitor center for people to enjoy, which can help them learn about the bioacoustic world.

Photos can be taken in a fraction of a second whenever there is available light. Videos can be shot in the time it takes to scan an impressive vista. Unlike photography or shooting video, however, recording enough sound to establish the signature of a particular location requires a bit of time and patience, but except for possible human interruptions it is no more difficult. Whether you're listening mindfully or recording, you may need fifteen minutes or more to determine the collective signature sounds that sufficiently define a site. Recorded sound, like digital photographs or video, gives you instant results. You can immediately play back what you've recorded. This allows you to decide if you want to record more. Bandwidth is now pretty inexpensive, and whether you resolve to collect individual sounds or the soundscapes of entire habitats, once you get your first sound and play it back, I predict you will be hooked and, like me, will want to get back into the field at every opportunity.

A Word About Costs

As with any endeavor involving technology, costs can vary depending on the quality of sound you want to achieve in your new avocation. For less than $200, you can assemble a credible, easy-to-use, pocket-sized digital system that you can take into the field to capture hours of decent recordings. If and when you feel ready to commit more time and resources and feel the need to upgrade, you can spend north of $7,500 for the components necessary for a truly fine system. The difference in quality and flexibility between high-end and consumer technologies is still noticeable and quantifiable, although the gap is closing. Of course, there many mid-range combinations that work pretty convincingly. Sometimes the system I choose to use in the field is made up of components that cost less than $1,200. At other times, I bring into the field nearly $10,000 worth of gear. It all depends on the outcome I desire.

Overcoming Techno-Fear

If you can take a picture with your smartphone, use a remote control to access your media devices, warm up coffee in your microwave oven, text or use Twitter or Facebook, start a fire, feed your cat, or scratch your head, you will have no problem recording natural soundscapes.

Despite my own dread of technology, I've found that the use of simple recording equipment enhances my experience of the natural wild in ways that viewing landscapes alone never could. At first glance, images of rainforest vegetation look green and dense and pretty much the same from place to place to the untrained eye. On the other hand, field recordings distinguish these locations through soundscapes as varied and dynamic as the contrast between the personalities of the Marx brothers and the Koch brothers. (To quote Groucho: "Outside a dog, a book is a man's best friend; inside a dog, it's too dark to read.") Nothing is as emblematic of a sense of place as a natural soundscape recording.

The words I will use to introduce the technology may seem a little strange at first, but the equipment is actually simple to use. Recording will bring you many pleasurable moments both in the field and back home. You may have questions about how to achieve better sound quality or on specifics about your equipment. Many sources are available to help you drill down to more, ever-changing particulars. You will find those featuring more of a balance between the capture of whole soundscapes and single-species models in the Further Resources and Bibliography sections at the back of the book. In particular, there is a free online help group made up of folks ranging from total neophytes to hardline professionals eager and willing to answer most questions you may have; everything from currently available equipment to unusual places to record locally, regionally, or even internationally. It is called NatureRecordists, and you can register free through naturerecordists@yahoogroups.com or contact us at info@wildsanctuary.com. The Nature Sounds Society, another fine source, is based in San Francisco and offers several great introductory field workshops throughout the year at nominal cost to participants. They can be reached through their web site at www .naturesounds.org. In addition, there are a few outfitters and guides that regularly feature sound expeditions to various sites throughout the world. There are also professional individuals who offer terrific workshops at various times of year. Martyn Stewart, one of the world's leading field recordists who has worked with the BBC and is a fine naturalist, frequently leads weekend workshops in Seattle. His workshops can be found at http://naturesound.org/nature-sound-workshop (not to be confused with the Nature Sounds Society address).

Now that you have learned how hearing works, and are overcoming your fear of the technology, I am going to introduce you to a few easy recording techniques.

First, most recorders have controls that are easy to understand. To record, make sure that your microphone(s) and recorder have fresh batteries. Since all equipment is slightly different, familiarize yourself with the manual and controls for the type of equipment you have purchased. And, most important, spend some quality time acquainting yourself with the equipment. Practice. Practice. Practice. Become so familiar with your gear that you can operate it blindfolded with confidence. It will be the best time you've ever spent, because you want this gear to be an extension of your ears and not a distraction.

Here are the basic steps for creating your first sound recording:

1. Assuming that your recorder doesn't already come with mics attached, plug the microphone cable into the "mic input" of your recorder. (Some recorders give you a choice of "line input," as well. If your microphone has a battery in it, try the line input first.) Make sure that your mic is switched "on."
2. Plug your earphones into the input on your device marked with either a symbol of earphones or text.
3. Set your input levels by hitting the "Record" button once on the device to put it into "Record-Pause." Then speak into it in a conversational voice with the microphone pointing at your mouth

from arm's length. Set the input level control so that the meter peaks at about −12dB on its scale. This will give you a practical recording level for most natural soundscapes.

4. With the earphones on, press "Record" again, and you should see the timer in the recorder data window advance as you are now recording.

5. Press the "Stop" button when you wish to end the sequence.

Play back what you've recorded:

1. Reset the audio clip to the beginning of the segment you have just recorded.

2. Press the "Play" button and listen to your recording.

Slating Your Recordings

A voice recording at the head or tail of each audio clip—one that provides minimal metadata of time, date, weather, location, and other relevant pieces of useful information—is key to good recordkeeping and assures that you don't forget what you've recorded.

Here is the information that I use for my template; all recordings should include this info slated either at the head or tail of each cut:

• Location: (site and GPS coordinates)
• Elevation:
• Date:
• Time: (in military hours, such as 0700)
• Recorder brand and model: (e.g., Olympus LS-7, LS-14, Zoom H6n, Sound Devices 702, 722, 744, 766, or 788, etc.)
• Sampling and bit rate: (for example 44.1 kHz/24bit, or other)
• Take number:

- Microphone: (internal or external, stereo, MS, parabolic, etc.)
- Recordist:
- Temperature: (if known)
- Wind: (none, light, moderate, heavy)
- Humidity: (if known)

Print out these headings in large type so you can see them better in low light. (I take my template with me every time I go out to record and am religious about going through the entire protocol.) If you happen to recognize birds during the process of your recording, tail-slate them (speak their names before ending the audio clip), and add any relevant detail at the end of the recording that was missing at the outset. In addition to your notebook, it's always good to have a backup record of anything you see or hear. If you happen to forget to do both, no worries. There are many folks in the NatureRecordists group who know most of the vocalizations.

Take Field Notes

As part of the recording process and to keep track of what you have recorded, be sure to maintain a journal of field notes. It not only allows you to relive and revisit moments you've cherished, it is also an essential step in the process of becoming a successful natural sound recordist. How many times have you looked at old family pictures but have no idea who's who? A field journal helps to avoid this problem. Good friends of ours, Ginny and Fred Trumbull, recorded in wild habitats all across North America and Hawaii from the late 1940s until well into their later years in the 1990s, capturing on tape large amounts of wonderful monaural data. When they died, and their collection was sent to Dan Dugan, head of the Nature Sounds Society, to archive, there were no proper notes on the tape boxes identifying what to expect and when on the hundreds of tapes in the collection. Without the Trumbulls, this left nearly five decades of work virtually useless.

There are a number of graphic insect, amphibian, and reptile field guide books. And, increasingly, there are a number of audio CDs, apps, and online references that are really great sources for identifying amphibians, birds, and mammals. If you are unsure of a particular sound you have recorded and can't find a proper reference, have your recordings reviewed by a naturalist who is familiar with local fauna. Any information you can provide in your journal will make archiving more exact and potentially more useful. There will be more information related to this subject in Chapter 10.

6

Equipment in a Nutshell

Because there are so many types of recording systems in all kinds of price ranges, and because new models are being introduced almost weekly, I'm only going to present here a generalized overview and some criteria by which to make your decisions. To facilitate matters further, we are establishing a web site that will constantly be updated by members of naturerecordists@yahoogroups.com, which you can easily join and contribute information to.

The simplest system consists of the equivalent of point-and-shoot video technologies, like a smartphone. But the first thing you have to consider is what you want to record. The second ponderable is what you want to do with your recording once you have captured the sound.

Each complete system consists of a set of mics (assuming you want to record in stereo or any of the stereo extensions, which I'll explain in a moment), a recorder with a decent preamplification component so that you are able to record the greatest amount of detail with the least amount of electronic noise introduced by either the mics or the recorder's electronics, and finally, a set of earphones or ear buds to monitor what your mics are picking up and sending to the recorder.

Today's improved equipment is so well designed and compact that many, like me, who have mild to severe technophobia or are unfamiliar with this type of gear, and who still think of recording as complicated and exotic, really need to reconsider. The professional field system I use the most weighs around ten pounds and consists of three elements: a mic system, recorder, and earphones (plus tripod and a mic cable). If you love the experience of being present in natural world environments as I do, this is the best field gear investment you'll ever make.

I have been mindful of the fact that wherever equipment is recommended, it needs to be reasonably priced, light, compact, easy to set up, and otherwise simple to use.

Remember, just as cameras have many different types of lenses used to capture different images, recording often benefits from an assortment of different mics to capture different acoustic perspectives. The language for all lenses is common, whether they are telephoto, zoom, micro, or macro lenses. Mics serve many similar purposes— only they capture everything from individual creature voices to entire soundscapes. Obviously, the best systems to use are those that replicate, as closely as possible, what your mind's ear desires to pick up naturally from any environment.

Microphones

Microphone technology is designed to detect and transmit sound to a point of amplification where it can be heard. There are several types of microphones, which are more technically called input transducers. Some are designed for recording terrestrial events, others for marine environments. I'll stick to the basics here, meaning simple, commonly used equipment.[1] Each type is designed with a different specialty and pattern that determines how it will receive and distinguish sound. For instance, *omnidirectional* mics pick up sound from all

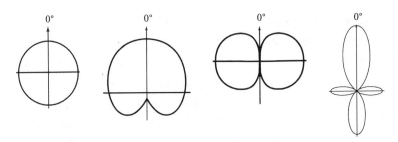

9. Microphone recording patterns: omnidirectional, cardioid,
figure eight, shotgun

directions equally (figure 9). *Cardioid* mics gather sound in a kind of heart-shaped pattern (hence the name), ranging from hypercardioid (quasi-directional) to cardioid (approaching omnidirectional). *Shotgun* mics have a very narrow pattern that can pick up individual sounds at some distance from where the mic is pointed (hence the name), while at the same time canceling out sounds coming from the side.

On occasion you might want to record in *monaural*—meaning that a single microphone is used to pick up sound within the scope of its pattern and level of sensitivity. Others are *stereo:* they consist of one mic with two pickup elements or a pair of mics designed to deliver a phase-related two-channel result. Stereo inputs receive sound from a two-dimensional panorama that generates an illusion of depth, movement through space, and (in some cases) direction. The four patterns noted here represent the ways in which the signal (the sound you wish to record) is gathered from the center of the crosshairs facing the top, or where a microphone would typically be pointed. In the omnidirectional mic, sound is gathered equally in all directions, 360 degrees from the center of the crosshairs. In the cardioid pattern, sound is gathered mostly from the front half of the space. The figure-eight pattern has lobed arrays to the left and right of center, gathering signals primarily from the sides. In the shotgun pattern, sound is received primarily from where the mic is pointed.

Monaural

Monaural systems are designed to capture sounds from a single source recorded and played back on a single channel. These sources may range from individual creature voices to the soundscape of an entire habitat. For that purpose, almost any single microphone will do. For instance, you can choose a shotgun mic, which is highly directional, an omni, or a cardioid.

Stereo

The stereo concept was described and patented by an audio engineer, Alan Blumlein, working at EMI in the United Kingdom in the early 1930s. While several different types of stereo systems exist, only three are considered here because they are the most common and easiest to use. From simple to more complex they are XY, binaural, and M-S. Each of these systems uses two monaural mics, either of the same type (as with XY or binaural) or different types in combination (M-S, also referred to as mid-side). Single mics are made that contain two mic elements internally, in an M-S or XY arrangement.

XY

XY systems usually consist of two cardioid (or hypercardioid) microphones placed at a ninety-degree angle, nose-to-nose, in a coincidental relationship to each other (figure 10). Looking at the setup from the top, the right mic picks up sound from the left side, where it is aimed, and the left mic picks up sound from the right. The sound

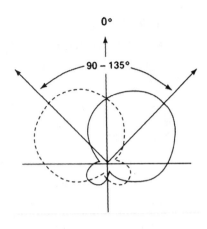

0°

90 – 135°

10. XY mic pattern (using two
cardioid-pattern mics)

from the left-hand mic usually goes into the right input channel of a
recorder, and the sound from the right-hand mic is usually directed
to the left input recorder channel.[2]

Binaural

Binaural is an expanded stereo technique that implies a spatial
recording illusion similar to what we hear with our ears. In the most
rigorous case, a model of a human head is used—in some cases with
a bust of the upper body and head. Small, high-quality omnidirectional mic capsules are implanted in the ear canals of each ear in the
dummy head. (There is even a combo system consisting of ear buds
and mics where the mics are implanted directly in *your* ears.) Binaural miking techniques are the only ones that claim to capture and
preserve all the three-dimensional spatial cues that our ears rely on.
In other words, binaural is ultimately resonant with the principles of
human psychoacoustics.[3] In the past, binaural results have actually
fallen short of our expectations, even with the use of headphones, but
new analog and digital playback technologies deliver more realistic

acoustic results. Usually these systems are quite expensive. Nevertheless, a credible binaural result can also be accomplished with a less expensive system. You can experiment with this by tying a piece of string around a tree about the diameter of the distance between your ears. Clip two omnidirectional lavaliere mics (tiny mics that are commonly used by TV newscasters and clipped on to their jackets or ties) opposite each other at the widest point. Mics of this type begin at around $30 to $50 and are available at many pro and semipro electronics retailers. Telinga Clip-Ons that are quiet enough for soundscape recording cost about $500 a pair. Binaural recordings made with this method have impressed even the most hardened tech-freak professionals who swear by the more expensive binaural gear. (More on this subject in Chapter 11.) If you can hold your head motionless for a long enough time, the lavalieres can even be attached to the stems of your glasses or the rim of your hat or clipped to your shoulders. Breathe very quietly and just be sure that you don't rub against the thin cables. As with other head-mounted mics, you'll get not only great binaural sound but also a stiff neck and a wonderful excuse to visit your chiropractor. (Lang Elliott, a naturalist and premier field recordist, offers a more comprehensive understanding of binaural recordings in the Appendix.)

M-S

The mid-side (M-S) system is unlike the others described above in that it combines two *different* types of microphones in one assemblage. My favorite system, it furnishes the recordist with five options in the results from one recording. It is also the most complex to use and the least intuitive. This semipro and professional-level technology requires some special consideration to use effectively.

Because of the nature of the M-S system, unless you incorporate special monitoring technology, or use mics or recorders that internally convert the M-S signal into stereo, what you hear coming through your headphones is quite different from what you experience with your ears alone. Some of the best natural sound recordings are made using just such a system, and many recordists feel that this technique is worth all the effort, although this is clearly a matter of personal taste (as are all recording choices). Others favor M-S for its flexibility in post-production.

Here's how a typical M-S system is set up. Sometimes one mic (usually the cardioid or hypercardioid) is piggybacked on top of a second, figure-eight-patterned mic, and both are set in a special *shock mount* to eliminate vibrations. The top cardioid or hypercardioid mic pattern provides some directional center pickup while the bottom figure-eight mic picks up all of the related ambient material in the surrounding environment, except from the rear (figure 11). Some current technologies combine the mid and side mic elements in a single cylindrical unit that automatically encodes the signal into stereo. This

11. M-S (mid-side) mic pattern (using one cardioid and one figure-eight mic)

allows you to record a stereo result from your recorder while monitoring with headphones, obviating the need for an outboard preamp.[4] The output from the mid mic usually goes into the left input channel of the recorder, and the side output goes into the right channel.

The mid-side system is highly versatile, which means you can achieve five very different kinds of results.

1. The cardioid or hypercardioid microphone (M) provides some directionality, which you can use independently to record individual creature voices.
2. The figure-eight-patterned mic (S) records a synchronous ambience that provides relevant information related to the creature voices picked up by the cardioid mic.
3. By combining both the M and S signals into a mixing matrix either in the field or in the studio you can achieve a robust stereo outcome that is extremely dynamic compared with other types of stereo systems.[5]
4. After processing the original recorded data through an M-S matrix to derive stereo, the recordist can obtain the most dynamic surround result from almost any surround system encoder, such as Dolby Pro Logic II, Music mode.
5. And finally, assuming that you do not signal process the audio recording (that is, equalize or mess with the levels), the recordist or producer can decode the M-S stereo mix, reversing the procedure, to get an exact duplication of the original M-S recording (using a matrix or multitrack mix software).

Hydrophones

Hydrophones are designed to record underwater, in saltwater marine environments or lakes and ponds (figure 12). Fully functional

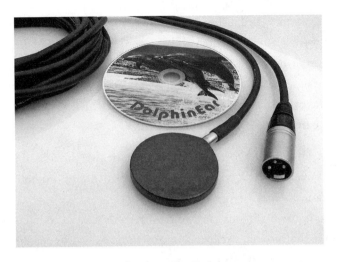

12. Hydrophone, by Dolphinear

models can be had inexpensively for around $30 or purchased completely assembled beginning at around $150. More expensive models can cost upward of several thousand dollars but are neither practical nor particularly useful unless one is doing serious research that requires careful calibration. Because of their excellent low-frequency response, we have been able to record elephant and hippo infrasound in air; very few reasonably priced microphones are able to capture this range of sound. We have buried hydrophones under the sand to record the singing of the dunes. We have also recorded the signatures of earthworms crawling through the soil with these instruments.

Parabolic Dishes

Parabolic dishes are used primarily to focus and capture the sounds of single creatures from relatively long distances. To my ear, under most circumstances the good ones provide better definition than shotgun mics but are more awkward to use in the field—especially the large acrylic or plastic models. They usually range from about a foot in diameter to several feet, with the size you need depending on the frequency range of the creature voices you wish to record. Lower frequencies require larger dishes. If the birds you want to capture sing in ranges above 1 kHz, a dish diameter a bit larger than one foot will do just fine: it can capture a full wavelength of sound at that frequency without a problem. If the creature voice is a type of mourning dove that vocalizes around 500 Hz, then the dish will have to be double that size, about two feet in diameter. If you are heading to Africa to record the low, guttural roar of elephants, you probably won't need a dish at all, because low-frequency signals are hard to localize. Theoretically, though, if you wanted to record an elephant's low-frequency vocalizations with a parabolic dish, you'd need one with a diameter of at least thirty-two feet.

Over the past twenty years, a Swedish company, Telinga Microphones, has set the standard with a truly clever collapsible and foldable system made of space-age plastic that expands to about three feet in diameter. One of these systems captures remarkable stereo imaging as well. This device is a fine compromise between shotgun mics and fixed-form parabolic dishes. The stereo version costs about $1,500. Because of their flexibility, quality, and comparative field reports from reliable pros and colleagues, the best parabolic dish microphones today are made by Telinga (figure 13).

The compromise (there's always a compromise to consider when choosing recording technologies) is that even the best dishes tend to color the sound to some extent, meaning that they might emphasize or attenuate some frequency bands over others. This is unavoidable if you want to extract an example of a single species among many. But to some extent, all mics color the sound, too.

13. Parabolic dish microphone, by Telinga

I do not own a parabolic dish; never have. My focus has been primarily on the capture of entire biophonies and geophonies, rather than single species. I have occasionally borrowed dishes from professional colleagues and friends, including those who work under the auspices of the BBC Nature group, Skywalker Sound (part of Lucasfilm), and highly skilled naturalist-recordists employed independently for field recording at the highest levels. I have relied primarily on their kindness, expertise, and feedback for this information.

Audio Recorders

Audio recorders are used to record, store, and play back sound. There are many new digital versions available now, and new models are being added nearly every week.

Digital recorders basically come in two standard storage formats: hard disk or flash drive. They are economical and easy to operate. Some require only a couple of AA batteries and can record for nearly twenty-four hours or more. Dedicated digital recorders (as distinct from multi-purpose smartphone types of systems) can range anywhere from around $200 to in excess of $10,000. It all depends on what (and where) you will want to record. Almost every one consists of the following components: a set of microphones or mic inputs, preamplifiers for amplifying condenser mic signals, a capture medium (hard drive or compact flash) to store the recorded signals, and a headphone output jack. There are usually a number of controls designed to choose your recording format (WAV, AIFF, FLAC, MP3, and so on), the sampling rate, the bit rate, and whether your input is monaural or stereo (and, in some cases, more channels). Then there are your volume control to set your input level, and your earphone levels so that you can set comfortable levels for monitoring the signal being recorded.

Headphones

Headphones, often known as "cans," come in many types and brands. Stereo headphones that conform tightly around your ears and block outside sound are preferable. There are several brands to choose from. Like the recording technology, which changes weekly, information about headphones too requires constant updating. If you can go to a local audio-video store, sample a number of them to see which ones best meet your expectations, or contact NatureRecordists to seek recommendations. I prefer the Sony MDR-7506 model.

7

Dealing with Noise

One day man will have to combat noise as he once combated chol-
era and the plague.

—*Robert Koch*

One issue all recordists have to deal with is unwanted noise.

An eerie yet notable effect resulting from the security precautions
immediately following the disaster of September 11, 2001, was the
incredible quiet that temporarily descended over our small northern
California village. Our home is beneath the flight path of planes
arriving from all over the northwestern United States and Europe
making their final descents into San Francisco International Airport,
nearly seventy miles to the south. With air traffic completely grounded
for a few days after the attack, for once no mechanical sounds came
from the sky above. On September 12th as my wife, Katherine, and
I sat in the garden in the twilight, we could hear birds and insects
that we had never before heard at that time of year. At one point, we
talked about how we were feeling guilty for welcoming the absence
of jet noise and the incessant interruptions of smaller aircraft and helicopters. We sat there stunned by the previous day's events, the sudden celestial tranquility, and wondered aloud about the possibilities
of the nation slowing down, catching our collective breath, and ap-

preciating the wonderful natural blessings we could otherwise enjoy in our own backyards, if only . . .

I have found that I like tranquility—locations where there is some natural ambience present at very low levels, but no extraneous human-produced noise. One winter vacation very long ago, my parents took my sister and me to a snow-covered valley in Yellowstone National Park. From where we stood, an exquisite atmospheric stillness engulfed us; one occasionally punctuated by the calls, cries, and chirps of ravens, jays, magpies, and horned larks. Elk, deer, and other four-legged creatures had been drawn to the lower elevations for protection and the expectation of food, all of which meant that we could easily spot and hear them. In recent years, this beguiling experience has been shattered by the relentless sound of snowmobiles motoring through the valley. The magic is instantly gone, obliterated by the noise and exhaust.

In Grand Canyon National Park, the noise from tourist flights or the whistling steam train traveling along the rim breaks into any awestruck reverie one might otherwise enjoy standing above or below the chasm. In California's great Mojave Desert, dune buggies and dirt bikes shatter the landscape's stillness. I do not use the words *silence* or *silent* in this context. That's because those of us still lucky enough to hear need some acoustic reference by which to orient ourselves. There is generally some reference signal present to link us to the space we inhabit. In a completely silent space, like an anechoic chamber where there is literally no sound (the true meaning of *silent*), we would not be able to survive for more than a few moments without going crazy; the deprivation of all sonic information would be more than our nervous system could handle. To me, silence means *no* sound whatsoever. And except for a very few isolated locations (and some types of caves) where we can approach dead quiet, there are no completely silent places in the natural world. We bring noise with us everywhere we go: to the lake, jet skis and motorboats; to the seashore, audio playback gear and software; to the woods, dirt bikes and chainsaws; to the desert, dune buggies and four-wheelers. It seems that no matter where we try to find relief from the din of our lives, unwanted noise intrudes. So much noise encroaches on our lives that we fail to hear one another.

Power and Noise, Noise and Power
It's Hard to Hear a Bird or Flower

The most obvious symbol of the American dream of prosperity and freedom is the culture of noise we've created. As a nation, we are preoccupied with power and the machinery that provides us with illusions of might. Many people in policy positions share the cynical view of James Watt, who once said that "noise and power go hand in hand." Watt, the former secretary of the interior under Ronald Reagan, considered this a good thing, a sign of national strength and progress. To amplify his point, in 1982, he defunded the Office of Noise Abatement, the only federal agency mandated to deal with noise issues countrywide.

Beliefs like his get dramatized every day in our recreational activities. On many Sunday afternoons in August, some distance from where my wife and I live, the famous Infineon Raceway draws huge crowds for NASCAR drag races and their spectacle of speed and noise. Infineon is fully eighteen miles south of our home. Yet the roar of the engines easily reaches our home, and it does not even travel in a straight line; it traverses several ranges of coastal hills, valleys, protected wetlands, and a regional park to get here. The contests begin every five minutes or so. The engines of the dragsters are so loud that

I have recorded them well above the normal daytime ambient levels present at our property line.

A sound industry manufacturer's award was given in the year 2000 for the loudest sound system ever produced for the interior of an automobile environment. To hold the attention of young consumers, a music system was designed that generates a sound pressure level of 174 dBA—nearly twice as loud as a .357 magnum pistol being shot at arm's length from your ear, and a factor of seven louder than a Boeing 747 at full takeoff power measured from ten yards away. All of this happens *inside* a car!

Sound levels in movie theaters with new audio delivery systems are more than four or five times greater than they were just a couple of decades ago—often beyond the safe industrial levels of noise mandated by the Occupational Safety and Health Administration. The public demands it, is the film industry's justification for these increases. Meanwhile, my wife and I now use earplugs when we go to the movies, or we watch them at home where we can listen at levels that are far more comfortable.

Why is it that with all our technological objectives directed toward making human life more contented, we haven't designed mechanical equipment to be more quiet? Could it be that we create this noise to supplant the voices we've silenced in the natural world? Paul Shepard theorized that certain signs of pathological human behavior are directly related to the loss of wild habitat and our disconnection from the natural world. To him, the ever increasing and unwanted noise in our culture was a perfect example of the types of behavior afflicting us.

Shepard lamented the loss of creature voices over the course of his lifetime in the twentieth century as he observed the important role natural soundscapes play in our lives.[1] The Canadian composer and naturalist R. Murray Schafer also noted that human-induced noise contributes to soundscape loss in the wild; where it is done consciously, it represents a potentially destructive expression of power. In *The Book of Noise,* he too suggests that our noise-producing symbols of brawn—pile drivers, front loaders, jet aircraft, straight-pipe motorcycles or muscle cars, for example—overwhelm and supersede the natural soundscapes, including organisms of all sizes, thunder, wind, quaking leaves, ocean waves, and the shaking of the earth itself.

We Will, We Will, Rock You

That human noises have a direct impact on phenomena in the natural world could not be more clear than in the following incident. In 1999, the *Los Angeles Times* reported that rock diva Tina Turner's voice had been identified as the most effective way to scare off birds hanging around the runways of England's Gloucestershire Airport, interfering with the landings and departures of corporate jets, helicopters, and other aircraft. Airport staff had previously used recordings of avian distress calls and other predators to frighten the birds away from the landing strips, but they had encountered only limited success. When they switched to playing loud recordings of the famed rock singer, there was an immediate and dramatic reduction in the number of birds.[2]

Human noise can greatly impair the transmission and reception of natural soundscapes, as well as dramatically affecting the behavior of wildlife and humans alike. Even otherwise wild creatures held in captivity are greatly affected by their urban soundscape environments. In 1993, when a military jet buzzed Sweden's Froso Zoo, about 300 miles (485 km) north of Stockholm, during a routine training flight, the tigers, lynx, and foxes panicked. Some of the animals tore apart and ate twenty-three of their babies, including five rare Siberian tiger cubs. Trying to protect their offspring from the onslaught of noise, the animals resorted to infanticide.[3]

Little is known about precisely how wild creatures receive and process combinations of noise in their natural environments. And we are just beginning to understand the complex ways in which these seemingly random events affect natural soundscapes. However, the increasing loss of natural sound due to noise and the human transformation of wild habitats should be a concern of the highest priority. Research into the impact of these changes is only recently beginning to address the need to mitigate the problems. From what we can tell so far, improved technology necessary to do the studies, along with a cultural commitment to make needed changes, are beginning to make a difference. Nevertheless, studies from the field of soundscape ecology confirm patterns that reveal the disappearance of biophony from noise and habitat loss—issues that field recordists have been sensitive to for some time—but are now being addressed with more authority and dedication, especially in Europe.

Still, the loss of natural sound compared with its effect on surviving living organisms may be more profound than earlier thought. In some cases, dealing with noise may be increasingly possible through software programs that have become available. These approaches are further addressed in Chapter 11.

8

Editing and Troubleshooting

John Cage once sniffed at the idea of natural sound recordings that were produced with a claim of being somehow "pure." He felt that they were "found compositions," and that there was no art to them because they hadn't been transformed. Over the years, I had several discussions with him about sound art; this was one of several points on which we disagreed.

I believe that the biophonies we collect *are* compositions. That we humans didn't have much to do with their creation doesn't make them less so. Through the process of merely recording them, they are transformed. That's because every choice we make in the field is a form of editing, whether it's conscious or not. And that begins with the type of microphones we choose. Each system will color the sound somewhat and provide an acoustic capture signature (sense of space, depth, frequency, and dynamic range) unique to those technological choices. Because recorders are now digital, they tend to play a less qualitative role in the ways sound is captured and produced, although the preamps and analog playback electronics can and do affect the outcome. Once you have decided on the recorder and microphones you favor, you then have to choose a time and place to record, setting up your mics in a way that focuses and favors one direction over another, and recording during one temporal window of opportunity as opposed to another. Weather, season, time of day or night, and specific habitats are other choices that will shape the outcome of recordings. In temperate regions, for example, creature density in spring is much greater than in winter, and it tends to be more dynamic and vibrant during the dawn and evening choruses. Biophonies at night are very different from those during the daytime.

A recordist has more control over these issues than may appear possible at first. Here are some pointers that may help you master the field skills necessary to become a successful environmental sound recordist.

The quality and content of your recording will be a consequence of captured sound as it is processed through all the technology you use to record, mix, and play it back. Whatever you will record is certainly not "the real thing." Rather, it is an illusion—a partially transformed representation of what we experience with our ears alone. Keep in mind that the more care you take with each choice in the chain of events, the better your results will tend to be.

Recording natural soundscapes is a type of abstraction, because you get only what the mics pick up, which is different from what your ears hear. By the time you listen to a playback of your recording, the sound has been transmitted from your pick of a location, with its birds, insects, mammals, and amphibians, to the input of a microphone, along a set of wires, through a number of electronic components to your recorder, and out again to an amplifier and (usually) a pair of earphones or a set of stereo or surround speakers. All of the choices that make up this sequence of events play significant roles in how the result is received by the listener. To create the best illusion, you need to choose the best combination of components that comes closest to replicating the fantasy you expect or wish to re-create. Every choice you make when you record is an edit or a compositional decision that will have an impact on the result. The following sections will outline the effects of such choices.

Microphone Selection

In choosing a microphone, you are making your first—and likely most important—edit. In professional recording terms, there is no such thing as an unadulterated recording, so don't waste your time thinking it's possible—even with the fanciest gear. The moment you find an affordable microphone that reproduces the type of sound you like, you have determined your first acoustic choice—the first compromise (since no mic does it all at the same time). The various patterns, frequency response, and sensitivity calibrations all play determining roles in the consequence. So it's important to carefully test various models to be sure you have what you want and need in a range that you can afford. Choose systems tolerant of harsh conditions. If conditions are dry and windy, choose a mic system that may be less sensitive and includes good wind protection. Even the best field mics with super-expensive defenses cannot withstand direct wind gusts of more than six or eight miles per hour without producing some interference. Omnidirectional mics are less reactive to higher wind blasts. You can mitigate the velocity further by using a *windscreen*—a protective sheath ranging from a simple foam cover on the mic capsule to more elaborate zeppelin and fabric-type enclosures. Foam wind protectors come with almost all mics, although some products are more effective than others. In a very windy environment, like deserts, islands, or arctic biomes, where I want to record the effect of wind, I usually use a pair of lavaliere omnidirectional mics, setting them low to the ground (if not *on* the ground) in swales, grasses, or bushes where the gusts are not likely to overload the input. This approach is quite effective if you can position your mics under a piece of barbed wire or a piece of wood with a few snags that produces assorted tones, changing pitch as the wind velocity increases and decreases.

Under those conditions, I choose the system less sensitive to high wind (usually most types of omnidirectional mics). Each mic capsule is covered with a special type of wind-attenuating acoustifoam (a kind of thick foam rubber sleeve that fits over it). These are then suspended on a mount that protects the mics from vibration, with the whole assembly enclosed by what looks like a plastic (actually nylon) and acoustically permeable zeppelin, or blimplike capsule. This whole setup is usually mounted on a tripod. The zeppelin, in turn, is encased in a "fuzzy" high-wind cover that looks a lot like a one of the late Jim Henson's Muppets; this covering diminishes the impact of strong wind gusts even more (figure 14). Every layer of protection covering a mic input will affect both the stereo imaging and high-frequency response to some degree. However, these sound-quality losses can be addressed somewhat in post-production, once you return to a facility with the necessary frequency-mediating software. Some professional field recordists, like Lang Elliott, use a system composed of two omni-patterned mics, and also build special shelters to protect the equipment from the strongest gusts. This preparation works sometimes, but if it doesn't, don't despair. Even wind in the most formidable environments dies down at some point. Just hope that the creature sounds don't stop at the same time.

Rain and humidity present a different set of problems. If either is predicted, you might try using a microphone less prone to failure under those conditions. Suggestions appropriate for a wide range of atmospheric conditions and prices can be found in the Further Resources section at the end of this book.

14. Zeppelin and wind-cover protection
for mics

Location Selection

Each choice of location will result in a unique mix of creature voices. Be conscious of the impact that extraneous acoustic signatures—human or geophonic, including weather issues—have on your recording. You may or may not want to have these signals as part of your recording. The important goal is to find a place you like to record. It can be any type of environment. The exact habitat you choose doesn't much matter at this stage. In the site you choose, decide which direction to point your mic system. More often than not, I try to choose noise-free habitats (or moments) and point the mic system in a direction represented by the greatest creature density. Also consider the times of day or night you wish to begin recording. Remember, in temperate climates during spring and summer months, there tends to be more creature vocal density around sunrise and just before sunset, but despite the season, most times of day are represented by some level of biophony or geophony.

Recorder Selection

You need to feel comfortable with whatever recorder you choose. So be sure to test several brands and models within your price range and seek out suggestions from those who already own equipment to help you make that decision. Check the controls to make sure they're intuitive and easy to use. Budget will be a major consideration. Remember, when you make your investment, try to anticipate, as best you can, what technologies will be available in the future.

Something to remember about purchases: I've found that when I invest in the best equipment, if for some reason I find that it doesn't meet my needs, I can usually sell it on the Internet for roughly what I paid originally. Of course, keeping the original box and packing material is key. If you buy carefully and take care of your instruments, they won't lose their value. A pair of Sennheiser MKH 30 and MKH 40 mics I had purchased in the late 1980s, for example, I sold in 2007 for more than the price I originally paid.

Troubleshooting

Many types of failure can occur while recording in the field. Because most equipment is subject to malfunction for any number of reasons, you will want to prepare yourself for those situations. Here are some of the problems I have encountered and how they were resolved.

What happens when your mics fail? Mics can fail for several reasons: the most common problems are dead batteries (if they're self-powered), faulty cable, bad connectors (either at the mic or the recorder), humidity, and even particles of dust. Dead batteries are the easiest problem to remedy. A faulty cable can result from a broken wire inside the cable (often because it was crimped when stored or severed by mice because you laid it on the ground and the critters were looking for bitable objects to file back their constantly growing teeth) or from bad connections at either end of the cable. I usually carry more than one cable with me, and try a replacement first to see if this solves the problem. This is much easier than trying to undertake electronic surgery in the field.

If your mics are sizzling and popping with a kind of static, or just plain stop functioning, they may be suffering from excessive humidity. Dry them off and immediately place them in a warm, dry environment—such as a well-protected bag of desiccant, a type of silicate grain in small cloth bags that eliminates moisture. You can find these online listed under desiccant silica gel packs. *Don't ever place it directly on a heater or stove to dry it out!* (Bye-bye, expensive mic.)

Once, at a recording site in Kenya, my mics began to sizzle and crackle—a sign I immediately recognized as a humidity issue. I extended the legs of the tripod the mics were mounted on and lit a kerosene lamp under the legs, just to the side and beneath the mics, about eighteen inches below. I held my hand comfortably below the mics, only close enough that I could barely feel the waves of heat as they rose from the flame, careful to insure that the heat would just dry them out, not actually fry the electronics. A protective metal dish prevented the flame's soot from tarnishing the mics. This method dried them out in about half an hour and I was able to continue recording.

Mics can also fail as a result of bad connectors. When they become detached from the contacts, the signal will be lost. A bad connection can also result from defective inputs on the recorder. Outputs from the mic are another possible problem source. When this occurs, especially if it is not a connector issue with the cables, it is usually more serious and requires professional repair to mitigate.

Once, on a bioacoustic trip to southeast Alaska, an elderly client found herself some distance down the trail from her battery supplies, just as a Swainson's thrush began to sing close by. Merritt, being new to field recording, had forgotten to check the battery that powered her stereo mic before leaving the cabin, and it died after a few minutes. She remembered a solution brought up during a "what if . . . ?" troubleshooting session we had the previous evening. Headphones can actually be made to work both ways—as a listening and as a recording device in an emergency. Merritt used her headphones as an impromptu stereo mic system, and was able to capture the thrush's song in a very credible recording. The signal was a bit noisy, but she got it.

What happens when your recorder stops working? First, make certain that your batteries still have some power. If they're working, check to see what other issues might have caused the problem, such as cable failure, mic failure, your earphones came unplugged, the input or monitor levels weren't set right. Extreme temperatures might also cause failure, so be sure the recorder is neither too cold or hot. Also, make sure there is still storage capacity left on your recorder's hard drive or compact flash.

If those solutions don't work, check to see that the recorder hasn't somehow accidentally been switched into "Pause" mode.

What happens when your headphones stop working? Any wire can break or become unconnected to a plug. If you're concerned, take two pairs of pre-tested cans with you.

What happens when it all quits working at the same time? Take a deep breath and enjoy the view. Electronic equipment fails sometimes.

Elements that affect the equipment:

- Insect repellent. *Never* touch any nonmetallic part of your equipment with repellent that contains DEET (N,N-diethyl-meta-toluamide). DEET can dissolve materials it contacts, liquefying paint and defeating the special protective qualities of Gore-Tex clothing. If mosquitoes tend to think of you as a resource for food, wear latex surgical gloves on your hands. In the summer your hands will sweat, but the plastic elements of your mics and recorder won't melt when touched by fingers that have residual DEET on them. If you are like me—a source of liquid food for every mosquito within a ten-mile radius—there are now a number of decent insect repellents (and even some kinds of clothing) that are less toxic and more equipment-friendly.

- Moisture in the recorder. Almost none of the new recording technology has moving parts (except for those that still feature hard drives) or delicate transport mechanisms that draw tape across magnetic heads, so humidity is not the problem it once was. Nevertheless, it is really important to protect your recording gear from moisture. Too much, and it may fail. And many manufacturers will void your warranty if that is the cause. A simple ziplock bag with desiccant will offer some protection as long as it doesn't get condensation in it.

- Dust and sand. The switching and control mechanisms of most recorders are quite sensitive to foreign debris. Keep them clean.

Tips that will make your recording life easier (and can't be over-emphasized):

- Battery life: Always check your battery supply before you go into the field. Make sure every component that needs batteries has fresh ones.
- Electronic storage space: Have sufficient hard drive or compact flash capacity to cover the amount of time you anticipate recording. Always overestimate your need.
- Equipment: Make certain you have the right ancillary equipment (your checklist should include: recorder, right mic for the job, backup mics, cans, flashlight, slate template, notebook, pen, a bottle of water, rubber gloves, head net, insect repellent).
- Equipment protection: Carry a liberal supply of fresh ziplock bags and rubber bands or string (to protect your mics and recorder from moisture and dust) and secure whatever you use to something solid.

If you are adequately prepared, you will have a wonderful time listening and recording, minimizing the difficulties you might otherwise encounter. Basically, you need to record just one ambient sound to know how easy and delightful this activity can be. Once you understand the basics there is a wide variety of exciting activities you might try.

9

While Listening and Recording

Discover harmony where it is most deeply concealed.

—*Heraclitus (c. 500 BCE)*

The following activities are truly gratifying and will inspire you to do some real exploring, stretching the boundaries of your ear's ability to hear and your recording gear's limits on what it can capture. When considering what you might want to listen for or record, always keep in mind three things:

1. Your presence may affect the behavior of many wild organisms when you show up in their habitats to record. Because your arrival at any site will most certainly cause many creatures to take notice, care is important especially if you wish to get a fine recording. Patience, consideration, and awareness are keys.
2. Always remain conscious and respectful of every organism around you. Your safety and that of others may depend on this.
3. Federal and state laws are fairly strict regarding close approach and harassment of endangered or threatened species in both marine and terrestrial environments. If you are recording with a commercial or scientific outcome in mind, you may need to obtain a special permit to proceed if you decide to record within the boundaries of national parks and many state venues.

Many of you are already conscientious about your presence in wild habitats. While listening and recording are fairly noninvasive and harmless endeavors—much more passive than hiking, camping, rock climbing, or skiing—your presence will still have some impact on the landscape and the biophony. I'll comment on other effects your presence may or may not have as I introduce the following activities.

The following activities offer possible adventures based on a number of my own rewarding field experiences. I encourage you to explore even further. But, again, be mindful of the effects you may have when you enter wildlife habitats.

Singing Ants

Ants sing. Don't believe me? Place a lavaliere mic on top of an anthill, covering the main entrance. Carpenter, harvester, and several other species of ants are the most common sound-generating species to record in North America. Some will "sing." (Bioacousticians sometimes use the terms *singing* and *vocalizing* in a loose sense to designate a creature's acoustic signature, which frequently indicates stridulation, the rubbing together of body parts.) Often affected by impediments blocking the entrance holes of their nests, the ants will congregate to remove twigs or any obstacle that restricts their movement to and from their underground nests. Since this activity is natural behavior, I've experienced no problem recording them and observing how they gather to respond defensively under these circumstances. It will cause them no harm. You won't be likely to hear ants with your naked ears, so some kind of amplification device like a recorder and at least one lavaliere microphone will be required. Low-cost lavaliere mics can be purchased at many audio-video outlets. And there are even less expensive ones you can use for this purpose. Make certain your amplifier or recorder is switched on.

Singing Sand Dunes

If you happen to be traveling by or living anywhere near the southwestern United States, you are in a perfect location to listen to sand dunes singing. The phenomenon of singing dunes has been part of southwestern Native American desert mythology and recounted in Western literature as far back as the early twentieth century. In the journals of T. E. Lawrence (Lawrence of Arabia), "singing" is common at many dune sites located in the desert—some more sonorous than others.

To hear this phenomenon, climb a sand dune like the ones at Kelso Dunes, a U.S. National Park Service site off the Kelbaker Road, north of Highway 40 between Barstow and Needles, California. When you get to the top of the dune, kick sand down the leeward face and listen to the low moaning and groaning that occurs. If you want to record the effect, bury a hydrophone just under the surface about thirty yards down the leeward slope (the one opposite from where the wind is blowing) from the top. Or, use a simple stereo mic and record at the surface. Be sure to protect your recorder from sand by enclosing it in a ziplock bag. Wind usually comes up by late morning and lasts until early evening, so I'd recommend going early in the day (there are also fewer visitors then). If you are not careful, though, sand will get into everything. Once it gets into the recorder's controls, it is nearly impossible to get it all out—particularly in the field.

It's good physical exercise getting to the top of these hills, which can be three hundred feet high; you can also initiate a minor but resonant sand avalanche by sliding down the leeward side on your butt. The dune will burst into a very low frequency song that's both entertaining and informative to hear and record. It'll be much louder than you expect and will sometimes last for several minutes. Watch the input levels of your recorder if you are recording.

Not all dunes sing. Of those I know in the western United States, only some are what we consider singers, such as those at Kelso, Sand Mountain (twenty-one miles east of Fallon, Nevada, on Highway 50), Crescent Dunes (about fifteen miles west of Tonopah, Nevada), Dumont Dunes (sixty miles east of Kelso), Big Dune (Amaragosa Valley, south of Beatty, Nevada), and Eureka Dunes (Hanging Rock Road out of Bishop, California). Some commonly accessible dunes, however, like those at Stovepipe Wells and the Panamints in Death Valley, do not. From the research we were doing in the mid-1990s, it seems that the sound is generated by the friction created between two or more layers of sand that are drawn downhill by gravity and traveling at slightly different speeds. Each of the layers appears to have a different moisture content, and the grain size and shapes are somewhat consistent among the "singers," and different from the "non-singers." There are a few papers and lots of speculation, but no firm conclusion yet as to what causes the signals to occur or why.

Listening Underwater

Many species of fresh- and saltwater fish generate *acoustic signatures* by gnashing their teeth on coral or producing sound with their swim bladders or through the oscillation of their caudal fins. The result of large numbers of snapping shrimp operating in close proximity to one another is a noise that sounds something like static when you tune between stations on an FM radio. In tide pools by the ocean, lower a hydrophone into the mouth part of anemones to hear probing sounds as their tentacles explore the surface of the instrument for something of dietary value. It doesn't seem to disturb them; once they've established that the hydrophone is not a food source, they'll sometimes produce a burplike noise and spit it out after a few minutes before returning to their normal feeding. Barnacles, as they twist in their shells, and tiny rockfish that occupy similar tide-pool environments also produce notable clicking and scraping sound signatures.

Be especially quiet as you approach and leave these aquatic sites. Critters will pick up the vibrations produced by your footsteps from thirty feet away—even if you have rubber-soled shoes and are stepping as quietly as you can.

Follow Water from Its Source

Pick a well-known river like the Hudson, the Mississippi, the Columbia, the Rhine (Germany), the Seine (France), the Volga (Russia), the Amazon, or the Nile, and trace the route it follows from its source in the mountains to its outlet, recording and archiving each type of habitat along the way.

The river will eventually flow into some other river, a freshwater lake, or the ocean. Following its entire course will certainly take you through many different ecological zones and places you might not otherwise visit. All along the route you will hear variations in water flow, creature voice density, and human sounds, all of which are part of the soundscape.

Puddle Songs

Freshwater pools or puddles after a spring rain are loaded with insect larvae, tadpoles, and waterboatmen—and many of these produce unique acoustic signatures. These microcommunities exist throughout the world. The insect larvae seem to be most active when the angle of the sun is high in a cloudless sky, although there is some activity on most spring and summer days, sunny or not. I haven't yet tried recording in these pools during winter, but there might be activity then as well. At certain times of year, the cracking and groaning of melting or forming ice is a wonderful geophonic expression.

Listening to Ice

You can capture the sound of glaciers moving over land by dropping a hydrophone down into a crevasse. What you'll likely hear is the terrifying and powerful low-frequency signature of the mass of ice moving slowly over the ground and, in the process, forming the moraine—the debris field of broken rocks or sand left by the passing ice sheet. This sound is typical of glacial movement in many parts of the world. Remember, crevasses are dangerous. The gaps can close at an alarming speed and one can get trapped in a way that provides few options for escape. I discovered this one summer day while recording at the Hubbard Glacier east of Yakutat, Alaska. I narrowly escaped when the mass lurched and closed as I was climbing out of just such a fissure.

The calving faces of glaciers explode, groan, and grind with terrific force as they break away from the expanse behind them. These instances provide wonderful and dramatic effects also worth recording. Stay far enough away from the pressure wave caused by the ice mass plunging into the water below and play it safe at all times. You'll usually get what you need from a quarter mile (400 meters) or so.

Once you've done some of the easier activities suggested so far, and after you become more familiar with recording equipment, try some of these advanced sound safaris.

Seasonal Soundscapes

Follow a soundscape through a single season or through a number of seasons. Many habitats in the northern hemisphere express themselves acoustically in dynamic ways, especially from early March through June in any given year. Begin recording in a nearby park at dawn provided it is quiet enough. Record samples of your park soundscape once or twice a week every week during the spring for at least thirty minutes—preferably the dawn chorus (just before to after sunrise). After you collect ten to twelve weeks worth of half-hour samples, select parts of three or four recordings that best represent your chosen region. Align them in chronological order, and play them back to experience the changes in creature density and to hear the resident and transient voices.

You can also record samples from one site across all of the seasons. Keep in mind that a lot of these ecoregions are now profoundly affected by global warming and other human enterprises. And those changes are expressed through alterations in the density and diversity of vocal creatures in several of these habitats. If you're going to compare before and after events, just be sure to record at the same time of day, month, and year in precisely the same spot, using the same settings on your recorder, to be able to accurately note the changes over time.

You might also follow the route of spring as it moves from south to north over parts of the North American continent. In the late 1980s, I followed spring as it moved north, sixteen miles a day through the high desert of the West along with my colleague the composer and pianist Phil Aaberg, also a fine naturalist. We followed the 111-degree meridian, tracking the route many Native American tribes like the Hopi, Navajo, and Utes had followed during times of their vision quests. That route, sometimes referred to as Good Red Road, began for us at the U.S.-Mexican border in Nogales, and moved north to Madera Canyon in southern Arizona. We then traveled past several wilderness areas and the Hopi and Navajo Reservations, into the Four Corners region of Utah, slickrock country in the Escalante, Goblin Valley, Capitol Reef, past Salt Lake to the Gray's Lake Refuge area in Idaho, the Teton Basin along the western slope of the Tetons, north into Montana and through the Gallatin and Lewis and Clark National Forests, into the Sweetgrass Hills, and on to the Canadian border. Our plan was to stick as closely as possible to the meridian in order to record the sounds of the spring season in high desert country.

All along the route we camped and recorded samples of high desert environments. This path across the open expanses of the American West is full of acoustic wonders ranging from dead quiet, almost immeasurable by even the most sensitive scientific instruments, to violent torrents of rain and flash floods that erupt during sudden afternoon thunderstorms. In a place so quiet that sensory deprivation can drive a person nuts within a few minutes, we were startled one evening by the chirp of a lone cricket hiding somewhere in a nearby seam of slickrock. In other areas, where dense vegetation would seem to offer a range of creature voices, there were absolutely none. In some places where there were a few recordable wild creatures, their voices would be interrupted by the sounds of cows, sheep, roosters, or dogs heard from a mile or more away. Jet planes occasionally broke the spell of these fragile wild voices. Sometimes our batteries died or our tape ran out at critical moments. Keeping a sense of humor, patience, and a positive outlook eventually brought us the successful recordings we hoped for.[1]

Create Your Own Story or Journey

Follow the sun from east to west. Record dawns or evenings from different parts of the country or the world during a particular season or over several. If you have the time, inclination, and resources to travel to remote places, sample events at the equator traveling the globe in either direction. Walk the crest of the Appalachians in the eastern United States, or the Pacific Crest Trail in the Sierra Nevada in California, or the Ruby Mountains in eastern Nevada. Follow historical routes like that of Lewis and Clark's journey from St. Louis to the Pacific. Follow the 1,700-mile journey of Chief Joseph of the Nez Percé tribe where he and many other chiefs and related groups outran and outfought five American armies for four months in 1877. Their flight began in northeastern Oregon, traversed the Lolo Pass in Idaho, turned south through the Bitterroot Valley, across Yellowstone, then headed north ending at the Bear Paw Battlefield in Montana near the Canadian border. This type of exercise presents limitless possibilities and exciting vacations made all the more memorable by the sounds you have captured.

Species-Specific Recordings

Birdsong is the most commonly recorded natural sound. These sounds have been traditionally considered "sexy" by collectors from the very first applications of recording technology. If lists appeal to you, just be sure not to limit yourself to birds. Record frogs from different parts of the country. Or insects. Or bats. You will discover that the song dialects of common species differ from place to place, and this alone may be of interest. Some recordists use playback systems in the field with an amplifier, speakers, and recordings of the bird or mammal they're trying to attract, attempting to lure creatures close to the mics to sing, do calls, or be photographed. I do not encourage or recommend this type of activity. (The ethical consideration is based on how strongly you feel it is right or necessary to engage in this type of interaction. If you have to ask the question in the first place, it probably isn't.) Generally I steer clear of baiting of any type for any reason.

In any event, I would encourage you to push beyond the common collections, and venture into new territory. Some species are very hard to find and require great patience and a lot of planning. Recording them may even involve special equipment. Aside from the usual parabolic and shotgun systems used for capturing the sounds of single species, recordist and naturalist Lang Elliott captures the vocalizations of birds and frogs, collecting them individually while at the same time providing a sense of the collective natural soundscape in which his target species can be found. He does this with a special mic system he has assembled that is referred to as a stereo ambient sampling system, or SASS. It is a technique that provides a result similar to binaural.[2] This type of species-specific highlight recording with background ambience can also be effectively done using the M-S system described earlier with the inclusion of a hypercardioid mic (more directional), replacing a regular cardioid mid component with one that has a narrower pickup pattern.

Attended Versus Unattended Recordings

There are generally two approaches to recording wild soundscapes: attended and unattended. As you might expect, attended recordings are made with the recordist actually within sight or short walking range of an operational recorder at all times. Unattended recording means that the recordist sets up the equipment in the field and leaves the site for extended periods to engage elsewhere. With attended recordings the recordist is actively engaged in the process whenever the recorder is gathering data, noting events that occur by listening to them unfold over whatever period they are transpiring. I prefer attended recording. I enjoy the process of actually recording on site because it helps me relax. The data sets tend to be smaller, but they are more manageable (for me). Unattended recordings are made with gear that can capture data anywhere from twenty-four hours to as long as two weeks or a month.[3] A process generally favored by more serious bioacoustic researchers, this can also be done with multiple recording units spread across a wide biomic expanse. This technique has the advantage of monitoring events over extended periods. What you give up in detail, you make up in quantity. The downside of large amounts of data is how to listen to it all. The problem is best expressed by an encounter I once had in the mid-2000s with a colleague. I was telling him how proud I was of the fact that (by that time) I had collected about 4,500 hours of soundscapes over a period of about forty years. Without missing a beat, and sounding pretty competitive, he said, "What do you mean? Last month alone, with eight remote self-activating recording units at one location, we captured over 5,700 hours of data!" After taking that in for a moment, I had the presence of mind to respond, "If one of your interns listened to every minute of your recordings eight hours a day every day during a normal working week, it would take two years and nine months just to audition one month of your recordings one time." Unpersuaded, he answered: "No worries, Bernie. We've got computers and decent software to do the analysis now. We can run the data in a few hours. People aren't even in the picture." And neither, I noticed, is wildlife. For my purposes, attended recordings work fine. It is slower, more purposeful, more connected. Without it, I never would have discovered the concept of biophony or the mitigation of my affliction of ADHD.

10

Archiving and Creating Projects

You've ventured out into the field. You've listened. You've recorded some great biophonies or captured some single creature voices. Now, you find yourself sitting among a large collection of audio clips trying to figure out what to do with them. There are probably some great sounds that you've captured, but how will you be able to find just the ones you want to preserve or need? As with photography and the inevitable pile of good and useless snapshots, some recordings can be weeded out while others are worth keeping; and, you will want to conform them into a pleasing and evocative expression of your journeys into the field.

Without a plan for organizing what you have, your recordings may get lost, erased, or plain mixed up, especially if you have a large number of files. Once these are systematically managed, however, the field recording excerpts can be "conformed" or "mixed" into a finished presentation. Whether you are planning a CD, programs on a memory stick, or a performance piece designed for other media, this chapter will guide you through the step-by-step process of organizing your sound recordings in a way that will allow you to shape them into finished pieces.

Archiving: Storing and Backing Up
Your Recordings

Too many great collections have been lost to floods, hurricanes, fire, wars, earthquakes, nasty divorces and separations, not to mention sabotage, vandalism, or carelessness. If only the scribes of the great library of Alexandria had backed up and stored their data, all of the vanishing antiquity problems of the twenty-first century might have been solved by now! So, while you have a chance, follow some simple procedures to archive your precious sound recordings.

The first thing you will want to do when you get home after recording is to back up everything you have recorded. Data storage bandwidth is very inexpensive now, so don't hesitate to make a duplicate backup to a good hard drive or other storage protocol. This is comparable to backing up data on your computer from the hard drive to another one or in the cloud to avoid being caught by a crash that destroys all of your records. I don't trust the medium (or myself) well enough to feel confident that something won't get lost, altered, or destroyed. My grandmother used to call this nagging element of doubt "healthy skepticism."

Be sure to keep the copies you have created in different locations (and that means storing one set at a completely different site, not just a different room). I keep two different backups at a location near where I live and one complete set of everything in a safe deposit box at the bank.

Recorded data is not considered safe or archived unless it is copied and stored properly, so you want to be sure your tapes or disks are kept in a cool, temperature and humidity controlled place where exposure to sun, heat, moisture, or other debilitating factors is prevented. It's a good idea to make a note to yourself about where you have stored each.

I currently use two types of software in parallel to note and link the metadata and audio files. The first is FileMaker Pro. The second is a system called Soundminer. Both are particularly useful and practical for managing large collections.

Documenting: Make a List

After you have your backup copy stored safely, make a list of what you've heard, and when and where you heard it. At the completion of any field recording session, I return home and replay the audio clip, referring to my field notes related to events that occurred during the capture of each file. You can enter the information directly into your computer, but try to do it while the field experience is still fresh in your mind.

As emphasized earlier in Chapter 8, your list of important information should include the date, times of day or night, GPS data, temperature, wind velocity, description of the site, length of audio clip, recorder, microphone type, recordist, sampling and bit rates, species (common and Latin names), and other useful "locator" information. Write down any sounds or vocalizations that you recognize and describe the ones you do not. Creature ID via information on the web is really easy to find now. So don't worry if you are not familiar with a particular birdsong. It can be found. If you don't know all of the creature voices at this stage, that is no problem. Even with a decent musical ear, I still have trouble ID'ing even the most common birds by ear. Later, you can return and reevaluate the material or enlist the help of folks on the NatureRecordists list. The more you information you can provide with your first listing, the easier it will be to refine and update it down the road. You'll also want to make some reference to the quality of the recording because it can help you decide which audio to use if you plan to generate some kind of presentation.

To the extent that your field notes are complete, you can then move to the next stage (other than the backup), the most important in the process of maintaining your collection.

Getting the Most from Your List

Once you note the creatures you have recorded, you may wish to create an even more detailed index. This might include information about where the certain birds or mammals appear during the course of the recording, as in the "Field Notes" section of your archive page. This type of information can be particularly useful for ID and retrieval purposes in the future. It is a feature that can be combined with your photo and video library as well, referenced in relation to what you may have simultaneously captured on video.

Using a template for organizing all of your notes will allow you to easily access your data, including the origin of your recording and any cross-referenced information that you anticipate may be useful (figure 15). Formats of this template may change depending on your goals and requirements. The sample described here illustrates the information one might incorporate. This document format was created with FileMaker Pro 12 software for Mac, but similar software is also available for PCs, and most programs can be adapted to suit your needs. As with any equipment choice, select a program you are comfortable with; it doesn't have to be complex to be useful.

Creating an Audio Library

Here are some categories to include in the archive information for a sound library.

Library_ID_No 1760 **Title** Zimbabwe 5 (1996)

DAT 410 **Prog#** <Field **Beg_time** 0000 **End_time** 1:27:20 **Duration** 01:27:20

Analog_Tape_No [   ] **N/R** <Field Missing **Cassettee_No** ....

Dig_Record_date [.....................] **722 Take Number** <Field Missing> **SampBit_rates** 44.1/16...........

Filename DAT410_PreDawn&DawnAmb.wav...................

BIOLOGICAL DATA:

Category Biophony **Biome** Subtropical

Aquatic_Habitat n/a **Terrestrial_Habitat** Riparian

Common_Name Ambience (dawn), Barred owlet, Scops owlet, Natal francolin, Freckled nightjar, Cape turtle dove, Ground hornbill, Egyptian goose, Bearded robin Baboon

Species (n/a) Glaucidium capense, Otus icteror hynchus, Francolinus natalensis, Caprimulgus tristigma, Streptopelia lugens (?), Bucorvus leadbeateri, Alopochen aegyptiacus, Erythropygia barbata Papio ursinus

Field_Notes Pre-dawn/dawn amb. **Habitat: low veldt kopje riparian.** Barred owlet (close) (40:16) ***** , 40:20 Scops Owlet, 40:28 Barred owlet, 40:40 Natal francolin, 40:46. Barred owlet /Freckled nightjar, 50:50 Cape turtle dove, 51:24 Natal francolin/Freckled nightjar/Ground hornbill, 55:59 Freckled nightjar, 57:42 Egyptian goose, 57:49 Freckled nightjar, 1:07:47 Spotted wood dove, **1:10:21 (43:28) Baboons echoing off kopje near-field w/ wonderful clarity dueting.***** 1:10:25 long bab. echoes ***** 1:10:00 Blue-eyed bulbul, 1:11:16 Bearded robin, 1:16:13 - 1:16:45 Fork-tailed drongo /Terrestrial bulbulYellow-billed bulbul, 1:21:33 Bleating warbler, 1:21:47 Hoopoe, 1:22:23 Buff-back shrike, 1:22:32 Bulbul shrike, 1:30:29 Afric

LOCATION:

Country Zimbabwe **Site** Gonarezhou **State_Province** [   ]

Altitude 579'/176.4m **GPS** 20°58'04.65"S/32°19'14.58"E

DATE AND WEATHER:

Recording_Date 9/30/1996 **Local_Time** 0422

Season Spring **Climate** Dry (cyclical)

Weather Clear **Temperature** 78F/25.5C

RECORDING DATA:

Recorder D-7 **Microphone** Senn. 30/40 MS combo

Mic_Pattern M-S **Source_Distance** <Field Missing>

Recordist Krause, B. **Quality** Excellent

Type Field Recording

15. Sample layout for archive information in a sound library

- Library ID #—Assigns a sequential number to your sound recordings; later, entering the number will give you immediate access to any individual file in your library. For instance, the first tape I ever recorded would be number 1; the most recent digital field recording would be somewhere around 4,000.
- Title—This is useful if it is a completed (or anticipated) project. For instance, all of the recordings related to my CD titled *Amazon Days, Amazon Nights* reference that title. Sometimes I just reference the location of the original recording in this category.
- Duration—This is the total length of a raw field recording.
- Digital Record Date—This also serves as an ID filename since digital recordings exist in that domain only (unlike tape or DAT recordings).
- Category—geophony, biophony, anthropophony, for instance.
- Biome—as in arctic, boreal, desert, subtropical, tropical. Aquatic Habitat: fresh- or saltwater environments, streams, lakes, ponds, marshes, swamps. Terrestrial Habitat: desert, oak chaparral, coniferous forest, and so on.
- Common Name—crow, robin, elephant, killer whale, or what have you.
- Species—the Latin names.
- Field Notes—special information related to the recording (not represented in other parts of the template).
- Country
- State or province
- Site—name of park, river, mountain region.
- GPS
- Altitude—You'll need a decent GPS, smartphone app, or heaven forbid, an actual contour map to gather this information.
- Recorder—Give the type of recorder, model name, and gain settings.

- Microphones—name and model of mics.
- Mic. Pattern—cardioid, hypercardioid, omni, shotgun, parabolic.
- Recordist—person responsible for the recording.
- Quality—This will help save time during production or finding a cut you wish to hear again.

Keeping Good Records in the Field

Keep a permanent record of your experiences in the field. This can be done as an extension of your field journal or as part of a separate catalog of your recorded media, or a combination of both, which is what I generally do. Information that has been carefully written down in detail can yield unexpected and useful material about particular creatures and sites or serve as an extended reminder of what you have encountered on your sound adventures. While recording one evening in Sequoia National Park, California, we had an exciting encounter with a bear chewing on our mics. This sound was recorded and noted in our journal, using the custom archival format we designed for the National Park Service. (Although this is something I wouldn't be likely to forget, the sound by itself might have been hard to identify a few years later if I had not made some notes about the occurrence.) Through careful notation you can always access what, when, and where events happened as well as your impressions of those particular moments. You can become an archivist tracking a particular environmental issue, for example, such as changes in the biophonies of a particular location over time. You can document evidence related to population density of a particular species, the health of a habitat, patterns of biophony as measured by time of day or season, or as related to changes in weather patterns. You can explore creature distribution, the impact of anthropophony on

wildlife as expressed through the biophony, the range of creature vocal expressions within larger biological communities, or biomes, and
your own impressions of being on site. Whether you are recording
for fun, to create your own autobiographical sound journal, to help
your local wildlife organization track and log species, or to help man-
age an environment under threat of development or destruction, you
will need to have some basic documentation methods. Various approaches to creating interesting and useful records include technical
identification and other indicators.

The methods for identification of sounds range from simple to
arcane. Simple techniques are those that include, for instance, the
identification and notation of the songs and calls of birds, voices of
mammals, stridulation of insects, and different frog species. My initial preference is not to get too stressed out when considering which
method to use. Observe what you can and take sufficient notes so
that you are able to piece the details together at a later time. Some
folks love detail. If this does not distract you from the enjoyment of
the moment, you might consider engaging at that level if you have
the field expertise. This includes identification of birdsong by territory, and notes on bioregions. It is well known that the songs of the
white-crowned sparrow (*Zonotrichia leucophrys*) vary from territory
to contiguous territory as represented by regional dialect. These dialect (expressions of song) differences can be heard with an ear that is
sensitive to subtleties of rhythm and pitch and by those particularly
knowledgeable about birdsong. Also, they can be recorded and an-
alyzed by comparing the acoustic representations on a spectrogram.
There are several computer software audio analysis programs that
are easy to understand and use for this purpose. Utilizing the same
method, you can compare biophonies from zone to zone, in the same
and different habitats at similar times of day or night and season, and

under certain weather conditions, and you can discover what remains consistent and what appears to change. In addition, and using the same analysis method, you can compare habitats before and after the introduction of human noise or before and after a fire, clear-cutting, flooding, or other natural disasters. In particular, analysis programs can indicate the ways in which certain creature voices might be masked or impeded, and help to identify the overall health, age, and well-being of those habitats.

Another popular way to identify is through structure. Again, from simple to complex, you can arrange data in many ways. For example, once, while recording at Gray Ranch, a 500-square-mile site formerly owned by the Nature Conservancy in the New Mexico panhandle country of Sonoran-Chihuahuan high desert, a colleague and I were able to acoustically identify many microhabitats within a five-square-mile area at altitude variations of not more than fifty feet (fifteen meters). Needing to find a data notation structure that could handle large amounts of detail, we used the archive information sample layout described above.

Your recording will never sound like the actual location did when you heard it with your ears alone. Every time you listen to a playback of a place you have recorded, you'll hear it differently and, in the process, probably discover something new. Your mood may have changed, your level of attention, your body chemistry, and other life experiences will all affect how you experience each listening of your recorded soundscapes. These recordings keep teaching us how to listen. Because they are so engaging, I listen to them often and, as a result, keep adding information to my archive log sheets. When I played a recording of a southeast Alaska soundscape for a colleague recently, he noted a particular bird that I had not previously recognized. I added the information to the archive log for that recording.

Keep your information simple and accessible with clear, cross-referenced notes. Finally, if you are doing many hours of recording or concentrating on multiple species, be sure to keep your archive up to date so you don't have to wade through piles of material because you put off the task.

Creating Projects with Your Sound Recordings

You will soon discover that a natural sound recording is worth a thousand pictures. No words or photographs can convey the power or dynamic of a place with more clarity. While slides or videos may vibrate with light, and film or video with the sensation of movement, soundscapes engage us at a different sensory level of physically resonant truth and kinesthetically take you back and connect you to the places you have visited or lived. A still picture of a black bear pawing my microphone may put a nervous smile on your face. Listening to the recording of the bear sniffing, growling, and then biting it creates a vivid image, and will make the hair on the back of your neck stand up. So, once you have recorded, once you have archived, what's next for enjoying and using your precious library of sounds?

Unless you are recording urban soundscapes, your recording will consist of species-specific (individual) creatures, or the more contextual perspectives of biophonies or geophonies (or both). At some point, you may want to produce an audio CD or other form of presentation for family, friends, or even professional gatherings. There are now easy-to-use technologies designed just for this purpose; they consist of software and hardware that can accommodate editing and mixing multiple stereo tracks. And they are readily available for both PC and Mac platforms. Among the range of editing and mixing tools, a few worth mentioning are Adobe Audition, Pro Tools, Amadeus, and for those audio clips that contain certain types of unwanted noise you want to eliminate, iZotope. Check online for the latest updates and tools because there are other good options, as well. Software is added or improved almost weekly. The following describes any of several forms of production you may wish to try.

Creating Finished Programs

One popular output of this work is species-specific recording. This method of recording single creature voices is used to highlight individual species. By isolating species from their larger biophonic context, you can get a closer sense of their vocalizations and learn about their respective acoustic characteristics. This form of production (bird-by-bird, frog-by-frog, insect-by-insect) lets you present the creatures' distinctive voices, including alarm calls, territorial vocalizations, songs, contact calls, feeding calls, and mating calls. It is particularly useful as an introduction to creating a sound recording "product" and is quite easy to do if you have the right production equipment and software.

Until recently, the best way to abstract a single species from the context of the biophony was to record using a parabolic dish. This is still a valuable method where there is a lot of ambient noise. But with recent software improvements, such as those contained in Adobe Audition, if the biophony is organized enough and there is sufficient spectral and temporal discrimination between the vocalizations of the species, just by framing the bird, frog, or mammal signatures in a spectrogram (similar to what you might do in Photoshop), you would probably be able to separate the bird vocalization from the context without having it recorded separately.

First, familiarize yourself with the editing software. While I've never created species-specific programming for a commercial album,

I have done it for museum installations. However, a fine example of this type of recording technique beyond the typical institutional models is Lang Elliott's book and CD titled *Music of the Birds: A Celebration of Bird Song* (Houghton Mifflin Company, 1999). In it, Elliott describes the calls and songs of the birds and amphibians in informative and loving detail. There are also other CD recordings of species-specific sounds, like the excellent compilation of birds of the western United States by Kevin Colver. There are recordings of frogs and mammals as well.

A second approach is to convey entire habitats instead of an individual species. From my perspective, recorded wild habitats have always provided a much broader soundscape context than the more traditional species-specific recordings. For that and other reasons, I prefer recording whole creature ensembles or biophonies. It is more expressive of the natural world as in general, and you can create dynamic sound mixes from those recordings. On the other hand, you could never re-create a credible biophony of a place by mixing a number of individual bird, insect, and frog vocalizations together. It doesn't work because, for one thing, even if you are using someone's detailed description of a particular habitat, the observer will still not be able to articulate with any degree of accuracy the density of the collective critter voice, or the distribution spread, or the spatial relationships that exist naturally. From my experience, you can only partially achieve that by recording the entire site at one time.

Using Your Recordings as Sound Sculptures

Sound sculptures can be created for many different types of media. This includes film, video, TV or radio broadcast, CDs, multimedia performances, public space exhibits, ballet and orchestral scores, and many other purposes. Recorded sound was first introduced to interpretive displays in public spaces (museums, aquaria, zoos) in the early 1950s, after the introduction of inexpensive monaural reel-to-reel tape recorders. Mostly, these early designs featured a single sound source and speaker system that typically performed one of two types of programs: push-a-button-hear-a-sound, or repeated extended linear sound loops that represented a snippet of a given habitat or even a single creature voice. The creatures represented within the soundscapes were rarely identified or even noted in signage. Basically, it was wallpaper music—sound introduced by exhibit designers for almost no purpose or desired effect whatsoever. Now, however, with a tropical rainforest audio mix, a dozen speakers, a surround amplification system, and many kinds of digital delivery systems, a dramatically forceful portrayal of biodiversity with depth and impact can be created along with informative, real-time delivery of useful and relevant facts about what visitors are hearing.

Sound sculptures apply the medium of sound in much the same way a sculptor thinks of giving shape to clay, wood, or metal. You can create sound sculptures to enjoy in your home or to give as gifts. They are soothing and inspirational to listen to and there are any number of occasions where a well-recorded sound sculpture will be a welcome and surprising gift for a friend or member of the family or even larger audiences.

In creating a sound sculpture, be aware of both negative (silence and softer sound) and positive (distinctive and louder sound) sound space to define and articulate the basic recorded material. You can mix elements to form cohesive works of art for either CD production or to develop a sound sculpture in a public space. Public space installations are used in museums, zoos, aquaria, and other venues, but the variety of locations and environments that might benefit from a sound sculpture is only as limited as our imagination.

Making Exhibit Installations

Once you record and archive a sound track you like, experiment with different ways to play it back. First, try a monaural system—one that plays only one track—and listen to the sound coming from only one speaker. Then try a stereo system—one with a two-channel amplifier and two speakers or a pair of stereo headphones—and listen to the difference. Then, listen to playback with an average surround system. With every improvement in the quality of the technology, the performances become correspondingly more powerful (assuming that you are working with decent recording equipment and have recorded good quality material to begin with). At the highest level, you can have your program operate with surround sound interactively with your audience.

For interactive performances, you can set your system up with two digital sources (CD players or computers) so that if, for instance, you are playing the ambient sound of a tropical rainforest and an audience member walks by a passive infrared sensor, it will trigger the second source to play the sound of a jaguar, or the sound of hornbills being flushed out of the canopy into flight. Your listeners will be captivated, informed, and delighted with the realism of the experience.

For interpretive purposes, long (fifteen- to twenty-minute) uninterrupted recorded segments are especially favored. If you have the software, you can create other performances from your recordings.

These might include customized audio delivered on memory sticks, hard drives for extended programs, or web site streaming audio (continuous long samples of sound perhaps with some video or other imaging) that provides ongoing, compelling, and entertaining views of the natural soundscape experiences you wish to share.

Combining Human Music with Natural Sound

For centuries, composers have been attempting to emulate aspects of the natural world and putting them into their musical scores, from Beethoven's Sixth Symphony (*The Pastorale*) to the tone poems of other Romantic composers, to Ralph Vaughn Williams's *The Lark Ascending* and Olivier Messiaen and other modern composers. Musicians and composers have tried to represent everything from the four seasons to birdsong, the wind, and the sea. Once you have a natural soundscape recorded, you might want to try to mix it with other kinds of sound—like prerecorded music—to see how it works. You may even wish to "sample" a particular bird, whale, or primate voice and use it as the basis for a piece of music you wish to compose.[1]

It is easy to get hooked and involved in making field recordings. Although analysis, archiving, and production take more time, all of these additional activities will help you learn more about these biomic communities and the sound-producing creatures that populate them. You will want to experiment and may need to dedicate resources such as a bit of money and time, not to mention incredible patience, to realize your objectives. Often, I will sit for thirty hours in one spot without moving in order to capture the sound of a single organism. What you're waiting for may or may not happen. Something else may surprise you. Yet you will be prepared to record it. You may not even know what you have captured until you get back home. It's all a process of discovering the voice of the natural world. Sound recording is a method of acquiring greater knowledge about the environments you visit. Once you have a good working knowledge of your equipment, the greater will be your success and the probability of great unexpected encounters with the wild.

11

Recording Production Techniques

My youthful isolation resulted in the love of quiet and retreats . . .
[I felt like] the animal who in general seeks hideouts and silence
because noise increasingly . . . represents the first aspects of possible danger and violence.

—*Loren Eiseley*

Art typically involves a process of transformation, as when raw
"materials" are converted into something wholly new. Whether one is
describing the process of change from wet clay to pottery, paint and
canvas to a visual image, letters in an alphabet to poetry or novels,
or individual dollops of sound turned into symphonies, conversion
is seminal. The art of recording natural sound is no different. The
composer and author W. A. Mathieu once wrote, "When you put a
frame around something, it's a picture. Any moment lifted out of
time is a photograph." What about a soundscape being lifted out
of time?

Once the pressure waves of natural sound reach a well-positioned
microphone, and then the result is converted in the recording process to bits of audio data, a makeover has occurred and a frame of
time has been placed around the recording. What appears within that
"frame" will be anything from boring to edifying, depending on the

choices you make; the sound recordist has a great deal to consider with regard to the quality and outcome of the final recorded product and is, in essence, functioning with the insight and abilities of an artist.

Here are some of the elements of a well-represented nature recording:

- A sense of depth and space. This is created by a robust stereo imaging (usually derived from XY, binaural, SASS, or MS techniques). If recorded well at the outset, the recording provides the listener who sits between a decently balanced pair of speakers with a spatial perspective of width as well as an illusion of depth. Care is taken to give "presence" to the featured signatures in the recording.
- Distinctiveness. These voices must be crisp and clearly distinguishable one from another; they should also be free from distortion and encompassing the kind of fine detail you might expect when looking at the feathers of a bird under a powerful magnifying glass.
- The artist (assumed to be both the field recordist and producer) has built content into the mix. This usually means that the artist has included creatures loud and soft, or ones that move through the acoustic space in the piece, to create dynamic and mutability over time. There is sufficient drama introduced by these particular supplements. Every healthy habitat on the planet contains these elements of expression to one degree or another. Because a field recording only represents a small slice of the real world this, too, becomes a kind of abstraction or representation. Therefore, any choice (or edit) the artist makes that he or she chooses to put into the "frame" becomes part of a mix.
- The artist has left his or her unique stamp on the recording. We each hear the sounds of the natural world differently. The ways in

which each artist chooses to represent his or her mix is unique. Listen for that special signature in the work. Every worthy artist has one. It is their special "voice."

- The recordist or producer's name and some information about where and how it was recorded are offered. It also helps to know the identification of the creatures featured in the performance.

- It makes no claim that the work is "pure" or "unedited." Every recording contains edits even if you do nothing more than choose to hit the "record" button at one moment and then the "stop" button some minutes later. You've framed your audio in space and time. Every natural sound recording, like other recordings, is a mix whether or not the recordist or producer had a hand in adding or subtracting the preferred ingredients.

Ultimately, it is up to the sound designer in whatever medium to hold the attention of the listener. The best natural sound art demonstrates an adept metamorphosis of the source medium—the field recording—into a new, finished work (CD or other media). Some sound recordists do this better than others because they thoroughly understand the processes of their craft and push its limits. The artist either will or will not produce stellar transformative results. In that regard, it is either greater, lesser, or non-art.

Developing Production Expertise

Natural sound recordings that were published and sold in the late 1960s sounded dull to me. Although marketed and packaged well, for the most part, these products were not only poorly recorded in the field, but badly edited back in the studio. They had all the earmarks of producers and mixers who didn't know how to listen very well and who didn't know how to capture the essence of the acoustic magnificence present in the natural world. Good or deficient, there has generally been a thirst on the part of the general public for natural sound recordings, inspired by the voyage to the moon, our growing awareness of "spaceship earth," and burgeoning environmental movements that drew attention to overpopulation, habitat loss, pollution, resource extraction, and other issues affecting the planet. Roger Payne's recording of the songs of the humpback whale was an overnight sensation and remains in print after nearly fifty years. There is clearly a need and a desire for credibly recorded natural soundscapes. Now more than ever, there are some superior products.

The primary goal of any natural sound recording I produce is the creation of an *illusion* that conveys a strong sense of place. This may seem like a contradiction because I begin with the conviction that a recording will never be the same as what you hear in the living landscape. It isn't the same. But sometimes you can accomplish an honest representation by simply setting up a mic in a spot and letting the recorder do its thing. Often, however, the final result will need some editing and, dare I say it, mixing. In any event, serious editing has already taken place.

The voices of the natural world are at once eloquently sensual and lyrical and any recording is, at its very best, a successful interpretation. In my work I strive for a characteristic result that expresses the dynamic power of that illusion, and I encourage you to do the same.

Sometimes you may get unwanted noise in your recording of an otherwise great take. In the past, the only tool you could use to try to fix it was crude frequency filtering that usually did more damage than repair. Today it is possible in many cases to restore the quality of your recordings through software processes. Adobe Audition has some wonderful tools you can try to help address those nasty little problems. Before you change any element of a raw field recording, however, be sure to make a copy. You'll never regret doing that.

If there is light broadband and constant noise, you might first try the adaptive noise reduction feature in Audition—assuming it doesn't generate too much artifact in your soundscape (making it sound weird). If the noise issue is really serious, you may need to look to more powerful software, like iZotope, for help. If there's an irritating mechanical tone throughout important parts of your recording—generated by a distant generator with a constant tone, for instance—the feature in iZotope to try is called spectral repair, which is quite handy for those types of issues. For low-frequency noise, such as wind, Martyn Stewart has devised a neat trick. If there are no other important signals in that particular band of the spectrum, he frames the section of low-frequency problem signals, and removes it. He then replaces the whole bandwidth with "brown noise"—a type of random signal that has more acoustic energy in the lower part of the frequency spectrum—pasting it in at a comparable level. Examples of brown noise can be found on the web at http://simplynoise.com. None of the higher-frequency components are affected, and the sense of space, stereo imaging, and depth is maintained.

Judging Quality in a Natural Soundscape

When selecting CD examples for reference, ask yourself these questions: How well does this recording command and hold your attention? Does the sound evoke a feeling of location and transport you there? When artists are passionate about their work, they ensure that great care is taken at every step to deliver on the high expectations that result when people have to shell out money, spend time listening, and procure the requisite delivery equipment to hear a recording in the best light. If other listeners (aside from yourself) are your target audience, then you have an obligation to deliver at least the first two objectives.

By asking these questions, you will learn to record biophonies that best represent your desire to remember and play as gifts to others. The richer in detail your work becomes, the more benefits you bestow on your audiences. In the process, you will necessarily find ways to reduce your recordings to the time limits of a decent product with all the necessary sentient elements intact. As you travel that route, here are some pointers to keep in mind.

Making Sound Decisions

With the raw field recordings in hand, you need to determine how you want to use your material. The ability to easily access your material will play a major role in this usage. So, first, archive your recordings with as much detail as possible. Your audio clips of long and short samples are typically saved on hard drives, some type of compact flash, or in the cloud. Once you determine how the mix will be designed for download or a product created for broadcast media, public space interpretive exhibits, sound sculptures, PowerPoint presentations, web sites, or interactive displays, you have a number of options to consider.

- How to use the concept of time—With natural soundscapes, time is represented by creating a mix that focuses, for example, on dawn-to-dusk chorus events or spring-to-fall representations. It can also feature a shorter period of elapsed time, like a simple dawn chorus or a dusk-to-evening chorus. (In real time, some dawn choruses take as little as twenty minutes, while others can last well over an hour.) As most of us soon discover, natural soundscapes can be seasonal, as in winter through spring, or summer and fall in a given habitat, or they can represent a complete annual cycle.

• How to use the concept of space—With movements from one locale to another, you can take the listener on a journey from the seashore on the beach, under the surface of the ocean, down into pelagic depths, then back again to the beach. Or you can follow a drop of water from its source in the mountains, then trace its entire course—the Colorado River, say—through multiple environments all the way to the sea.

• How to combine time and space—You could follow the John Muir trail through several seasons, or the route of Lewis and Clark, or your journey might begin with springtime in the valley floor of the Grand Teton mountain range, and travel north into summertime and the nearby bioregions of Yellowstone National Park. You might follow the journey of spring as it moves north, some sixteen miles a day, from a point in the geographical south along a particular latitude, all the way to the Canadian border, or even up to the Beaufort Sea.

• How to explore varied habitats within biomes—Some extreme locations, like the Arctic, Antarctic, or desert biomes, cannot easily be represented by any of the above examples alone. In that case, it is best to break up the zones and times into distinct cuts. In the album we did featuring nighttime choruses, Ruth Happel and I each contributed a representative recording of a spot in the eastern United States and one made in the Far West. Nighttime biophonies come from relatively small habitats represented in two different cuts on our album, *Midsummer Nights,* or, as Doug Quin did while exploring a wider ecoregion in his extraordinary album, *Antarctica*.[1]

• How to create a web site audio program—If you're into creating web sites with audio, MP3, Flash, and FLAC are common currently available download formats. By far the best current format for reproduction we've found is 96 kHz/24-bit audio. But you can't convert and upgrade your media after the fact (say, from 44.1 or 48 kHz to 96 kHz) with any benefit. To get the best result, all of your field recordings have to be made in high-sampling formats from the get-go. You can certainly downshift to a lower sampling rate from 96 kHz, though. The web is a marvelous medium for sharing your sound recordings and audio information about a favorite natural site. You can post your recordings on soundcloud.com, YouTube, or Vimeo, among others. If done right, you can give visitors an aural preview of what they might find during an actual visit to your favorite place—assuming you want to share that information. Or, you can create audio postcards to send to friends and family. Printed out, these might take the shape of an envelope the size of a CD (five inches square) with a graphic and an audio CD of a favorite location you have recorded.

We've just scratched the surface with regard to the kinds of programs you can derive from your recordings and the concepts to consider when developing them. It would take many more books than I have the room to write here to reveal all of the permutations. But part of the fun is in the discovery, and you now have a few tools you can use to begin that process.

In the final chapter, we'll visit some places I've particularly enjoyed and I will offer some insights about what I found there that you might also find exciting to explore.

The pheasant cries out from the door of its nest . . .
Crying out from the door, at the sound of the coming
    rain . . .
Rain and wind from the west, spreading over the coun-
    try . . .
It cries out, perched on the top rails of the huts.
It is always there, at the wide expanse of water, listening for
    the rising
      wind and rain:
Wind and rain from the west, as the pheasant cries out . . .
—*from Arnhem Land, Australia, on* Technicians
of the Sacred

12

Bioregions and Sounds to Explore

The world leaves no track in space, and the greatest action of man leaves no mark in the vast idea.

—*Ralph Waldo Emerson*

Marine and terrestrial environments are often flourishing with sound. Within these two main earth ecoregions, there are many transition zones called *ecotones* that feature revealing soundscapes. An ecotone is an area of progression between one type of habitat and another: from meadow to forest, for example, or coral reef to open ocean.

The exploration of sound reveals how many different types of rainforest, desert, and temperate zones can be characterized. Marine environments, for example, include ponds, puddles, pelagic (open) ocean, littoral ocean (close to shore), freshwater habitats, and still-vital coral reefs—each one revealing a huge variety of distinctive sounds. There are also transitional marine environments, such as intertidal zones, and places like mangrove swamps, coastal chaparral, secondary and tertiary dune zones, and island biomes. There are also many types of riparian habitats, ranging from small creeks that have very little water in them to roaring high-mountain rivers or the banks of the vast midwestern muddy waters of rivers like the Mississippi.

On land, there are numerous extraordinarily diverse environments, from the aridity of deserts to the lush tropics and subtropical areas, from broad prairie to dense woodlands, from arctic and subarctic areas to more temperate zones.

It is hard to name a favorite place among such diversity, but most of us have at least one or two locations that excite or engage us more than any other. For me, that place is Alaska, because it contains *everything*—from rainforests to some of the most exciting marine life on the planet. With nearly 34,000 miles of coast, it has the longest shoreline of any state. There are fewer than 750,000 (human) inhabitants (as of this writing, at least), which tends to make several wild regions within the state relatively quiet places to record. Part of the discovery of wild soundscapes is discovering what specific types of habitats resonate with you. Through the adventure of sound recording, you become more connected with those places and more aware of how intricate and beautiful they are. In this chapter, we'll explore a few of those bioregions with an ear to capturing wild sounds.

I will arise and go now, and go to Innisfree,
And a small cabin build there, of clay and wattles made:
Nine bean-rows will I have there, a hive for the honey-bee,
And live alone in the bee-loud glade.

And I shall have some peace there, for peace comes drop-
   ping slow,
Dropping from the veils of the morning to where the
   cricket sings;
There midnight's all a glimmer, and noon a purple glow,
And evening full of the linnet's wings.

I will arise and go now, for always night and day
I hear lake water lapping with low sounds by the shore;
While I stand on the roadway, or on the pavements grey,
I hear it in the deep heart's core.
—*William Butler Yeats, "The Lake Isle of Innisfree"*

Deserts

Some of my friends and colleagues prefer the desert. In North and Central America, desert regions stretch from the middle of Mexico north through much of Utah, Colorado, Nevada, and California. A great deal of creature sound obviously depends on each area's altitude, climate, and available food and water. Nevertheless, there are many vocal insects, birds, mammals, and even reptiles to be found in what some dismissively consider the most desolate of places.[1]

Deserts are mistakenly thought of as wastelands where nothing much happens. When automobiles tear by at seventy-five miles per hour, all the passengers see are flashes of occasional scrub and cactus set upon mounds of sand or crusted soil. Miners dig the precious ores buried in the mountains and caves. The military shells and bombs the landscape. And, some in the federal government and beyond think of deserts as perfect for the storage of the nation's nuclear wastes. Then there are those who find it fun to break what they think of as the desert's dead silence with disquieting dune buggies, dirt bikes, and overland recreational vehicles. But the desert is a fragile landscape. In many parks there, you are instructed to remain strictly within the borders of the marked paths that wind through forests of cacti and porous rock, because the diatomaceous earth is filled with microscopic life. It is also alive with the voices of many kinds of creatures and environmental sounds. But they're fragile and easily disturbed.

The Sonoran-Chihuahuan high desert is located in the panhandle of New Mexico. It is the only location in the lower forty-eight states where my colleagues and I found a completely noise-free habitat for extended periods of time. In two weeks on site, we heard or saw only one single-engine plane, and heard one pickup truck on the road early one morning. Gray Ranch (now privately owned and called the Diamond A) is a former Nature Conservancy property where we were invited to work. It is about 500,000 square miles in size. We concentrated primarily on a small area of about five square miles. Even within this zone, the biome contained many different mini-habitats, each characterized by distinctive biophonic subdivisions.

This whole area of North America is in the throes of recovery from several centuries of overgrazing—a place where older bioacoustic paradigms might not apply. The biomes with aspens, juniper and oak, mesquite, cactus, manzanita, alder, hackberry, shrub, Indian rice, sawgrasses, broom, sage, arrow weed, ocotillo, each feature their own mix of vocal creatures. During our visit it was populated by special mixes of cactus and rock wrens, common and Chihuahuan ravens, western meadowlarks, house, Brewer's, chipping, and sage sparrows, green-tailed towhees, blue grosbeaks, longspurs, loggerhead shrikes, vermillion and ash-throated flycatchers, horned larks, western kingbirds, common poorwills, burrowing and great horned owls, ground doves, aplomado falcons, red-tailed hawks, scaled quails, katydids, crickets, coyotes, gray foxes, mountain lions, jack rabbits, squirrels, bats, mice, beetles, ants, termites, grasshoppers, Mormon crickets, toads and frogs of many types, geckos, tortoises, and snakes. Each creature there had a singularly expressive voice; the environments in which they live are alive with beguiling choruses.

The desert—as with any biome—is a wonderful spot to learn to listen if you can get far enough away from roads, the water pumps of farms and ranches, the "grasshoppers" pumping for oil, the roar of recreational vehicles, and the sounds of domesticated animals.

California's Mojave is full of good recording sites and another great desert to explore. Some good places to start on a sound safari are campsites located at Granite Pass, on Kelbaker Road off Highway 40, between Barstow and Needles, California. The campsites are situated to the west as you come to the top of the pass from the south. From there, you will find accessible trails into the Granite Mountains. There are lots of birds, wild burros, and ringtails to see, listen to, and record.

Five and a half miles to the north on Kelbaker Road is the cutoff for the Kelso Dunes, famous for resonant dune-song. If you decide to record dunes, bear in mind that the dune surfaces tend to be windy; mics will not generally tolerate bluster unless their patterns are omnidirectional. Nor do recorders with knobs and slots tolerate sand very well. Another way to help lessen the effect of wind in your microphone is to introduce a *filter* into the line between your mic and the sound source before the signal reaches the recorder. By filtering out low frequencies below 100 Hz, the wind's effect, if it's not too strong, is greatly reduced. Some mics have a low-frequency filter switch as an integral part of the system that can be activated. Some upper-end recorders come equipped with a filter at the mic input or internally. And some systems require an outboard preamplifier with a filter included.

From the Mojave Desert, it's about 120 miles north to Death Valley Junction, an area I would not recommend simply because it is too well-traveled, and there are no booming dunes. However, my colleague and friend Jack Hines has made a wonderful recording in the park at both Mesquite and Anvil Springs.[2]

If you can find a way up into the Amargosa Range, which borders Nevada on the east and the Panamints in the west and is protected from traffic noise, you might hear some coyotes and discover many birds that frequent the area.

California's fascinating Mono Lake is set in the rain shadow of the eastern Sierra Nevada and is typical of a high desert bioregion. A part of the Great Basin, it is located just off Highway 395, south of Reno, Nevada, and Bridgeport, California, or through the Tioga Pass east of Yosemite at the end of Highway 120. At first glance it is an eerily placid-looking lake with magical tufa towers and is a wonderful but sometimes windy environment to record. I've recorded spadefoot toads not far from the hot springs at the north side of the lake since 1984. Until the mid-1990s, one could record there with no problem. But then the number of toads began to fall off, and it was obvious that there was something amiss. The Forest Service, along with volunteers from the Mono Lake Committee, rebuilt parts of the fragile landscape and vegetation by replanting native grasses and allowing more water flow, so that the toads and other wildlife could coexist throughout their respective cycles, replenishing their threatened populations.

Professional recordists may need to get a permit to record there, although no permit is needed if your purpose is noncommercial. The criteria change from year to year and administration to administration. At one point, the Bureau of Land Management and the National Park Service distinguished between commercial and noncommercial use by the number of legs on the mount under your microphone or camera. If you used a tripod, your purpose was automatically deemed commercial. Once, after getting busted for using a tripod to mount my mics, I returned the next day to the same site and mounted them on a monopod. No problem with one leg; no bust. Go figure. In addition, there are strict (and periodically mutable) rules about how close you can camp to the edge of one of the frog ponds.

One ranger from the Bureau of Land Management told me it was one hundred feet. One told me it was farther. Yet another said that there was no rule. Nevertheless, this area is worth recording as long as you tread lightly and remain conscious of the rules by talking with the local Forest Service rangers and reading the signage posted on the fences. Your recordings of spadefoot toads, a very unusual creature with great performance skills, and red-winged blackbirds, waterfowl, and California gulls will be something to hear! The best times—when there's been enough precipitation the previous winter months in the eastern Sierras—are from late March through early May.

The Ruby Mountains are located about ten hours east of San Francisco on Highway 80 (south of Wells, Nevada), and three hours west of Salt Lake City. It's another great high-mountain desert location. Get there early in the spring before other campers, hikers, and recreational vehicles arrive. There are two accessible sites worth exploring. One is on the western side a mile to the southwest of Lamoille. Take Forest Service Road (FR) 660 (Lamoille Canyon Road) toward Ruby Crest National Recreation Area to find lots of campsites. If the snow has melted, there may be other campers and pickup trucks heading toward the top as well, so noise might be a factor. Unless you're recording streams, though, you will find better and quieter places to listen, observe, and record on the eastern side of the mountain range.

There's a ridgeline hiking trail that offers spectacular views, good recording (when the wind is light), and not too many people. On the eastern side of the range you will find more campsites and fine places to record. To reach this area—accessible south of Wells—take Highway 93 south to 229 west; where the 229 paved section ends, keep heading south on the dirt road. Take any of the accessible Forest

Service roads (you'll definitely need four-wheel drive, a good pair of legs, or both), and head west up the hill to any of multiple campsites. For those who like to hike and wish to find great spring and early summer locations to record, there are many trails and terrific bird, mammal, and insect sites at this location.

There are, of course, deserts in many parts of the world, and because of climatic changes they are expanding rapidly. I haven't been to many offshore except for the high desert of the Masai Mara in Kenya, and Australia, where the Pitjanjatjara (aborigines) tell of finding directions from place to place by listening to how the green ants sing. If you have the wherewithal and the inclination to travel, try the Skeleton Coast in Namibia, Australia, island biomes, parts of the Sahara and the Sinai, and the coastal Peruvian desert.

Rainforests

North Americans commonly think of rainforests as steamy and hot, exotic, dangerous, and primarily equatorial. In addition to numerous examples in Africa, Australia, and Southeast Asia, however, rainforest biophonies express themselves throughout the Americas as well, from biomes way south of the equator in Latin America all the way to coastal Alaska. South of the equator, rainforests begin at the edge of Rio de Janeiro (although these have now been pretty much destroyed), and can be found in Colombia, Peru, Chile, and Ecuador. In the northern hemisphere, rainforests exist in Central America and along the coasts of Northern California, Oregon, Washington, and British Columbia, even as far north as Anchorage, Alaska. A rainforest may be "dry" (about ninety inches of rain each year) or wet, with hundreds of inches of rain, but even the dry ones are pretty wet.

Elsewhere in the United States rainforests and swamps exist in the southeast, from the Everglades and Corkscrew Swamp in Florida, Cypress Creek in Georgia, to the bayous of Louisiana. These are fairly accessible and exhilarating places to explore and record. Just be conscious of the dense populations in those parts of the country; those sites come with the usual aircraft, watercraft, and land vehicle issues. If you begin late at night or before dawn, you will find quieter and more rewarding intervals in which to listen and record.

Just north of Rio de Janeiro is an area called the Rio Doce or the Caratinga region, which is a dry tropical rainforest known for its large howler monkeys (*Alouatta fusca*), golden lion tamarins (a type of really beautiful tiny monkey, *Leontopithecus rosalia*), and the many birds and insects that inhabit what little remains of the natural forest. They occupy the last existing dry rainforest of a habitat that once stretched about fifteen hundred miles from south of Amazonia down to Rio de Janeiro. Reduced now to about eighteen square miles, this biological island has been designated as a research site. However, the boundaries of the forest are constantly besieged by farmers and others living just outside the borders who harvest the once abundant hardwood fuel and wild plants and animals with impunity.

Among the biophonies heard there are voices that include the pauraque, great kiskadee, rufus-bellied thrush, white-crested guan, common potoo, yellow-throated spinetail, tropical screech owl, spectacled owl, pygmy owl, black-bellied tree duck, slaty ant shrike, Amazonian antpitta, and the sounds of raucous parrot flyovers. A wide variety of frogs and several different species of ants also produce audible signals in this rainforest. As with many research sites, the biologists who built the place established one-hundred-meter grids within the forest marked by paths that lead one from location to location. However, the biophonic territories are shaped quite differently and do not follow the rational human structures we try to impose on the natural world. Instead, the territories are more amoeba shaped—sometimes as small as 100 square meters (about 120 square yards)—the boundaries are quite flexible and expand, contract, and change shape according to times of day and night, seasons, and weather for reasons we have yet to explain. It is possible to discover bioacoustic zones as large as half a mile or more.

Traditional research models often do not fit the true territorial acoustic boundaries of a site, so sometimes you must disregard what you see on a map and figure out the bioacoustic shape for yourself, paying special attention to the biophonies that define the margins. It is the acoustic expression of the entire habitat that sets the limits. This sonic charting is really fun to do, whether or not you are recording. As you walk through a given habitat, note the changes in the biophony—especially the transitional zones where one territory blends into another. There are regional consistencies you will begin to recognize—things that remain constant—and other sounds that will change as you move through the territory. This appears to be true for most biomes—not only rainforests. In this case it is the characteristics of the biophony that establish the boundaries.

Dry Forests of Africa

Kopjes (pronounced "copies") are large granite outcroppings—sometimes three hundred feet (one hundred meters) high—that rise out of the high flat terrain in parts of southeastern Africa, and particularly in Zimbabwe. Some dry forest sites in northern South Africa and parts of Zimbabwe allow sound to reverberate or echo off the kopjes, and these are favored by many vocal creatures. During the night, when moisture created by dew settles on the surfaces of the rock in what is called fringe mopani edge scrub vegetation, the combination of landscape and geological features will produce conditions where a reverberant theater is created. It is a place where several species of birds and mammals love to congregate to project their voices. On typical African spring mornings, you might hear a troop of baboons bouncing sound off a nearby kopje, modulating their voices in astounding ways. With loud, sharp, barklike vocalizations, they project sound toward the cliffs, then wait until the echoes of their voices die before performing the same sound all over again. Sometimes they use the reverberation as a duet mechanism, where one baboon will bark sharply, followed by another bark so that it can accompany the sound of its own dying echoes. I happened to capture this moment on tape one morning along with the sounds of a rattling cisticola, kurrichane thrush, green-spotted dove, bleating warbler, chinspot battis, buffback shrike, red-billed wood hoopoe, and a bru bru. An example of this type of biophony can be heard in the samples provided on the book's web page.

Reverberant sound projection occurs in nearly every biome except the driest deserts. Some examples include the predawn voices of hyenas echoing in the forest scrub of the Masai Mara, in Africa; the cry of wolves around Glacier Bay in Alaska; killer whales bouncing their voices off the cliffs of Johnstone Strait near eastern Vancouver Island; humpback whales trumpeting off Point Adolphus in Alaska's Icy Strait; red-tailed hawks on early mornings in northeastern Oregon; and ravens circling high over mountain lakes on early misty mornings in the springtime. Many times when I've been half awake listening to these ethereal sounds, the creature echoes give me the eerie dreamlike feeling of being suspended somewhere in a vast echo chamber.

Australian Habitats

Upriver from Port Douglas in the northeast corner of Australia is a terrific riverine rainforest environment, replete with vocal birds, crocodiles, ants, reptiles, amphibians, and crustaceans (including the loudest snapping shrimp sounds we've ever recorded). At locations like these you will find both enchanting and disquieting moments, as I did one afternoon when I encountered a crocodile and watched as it snatched an unwary poodle leaning over the riverbank to get a drink. As with other Australian biomes, this one is under siege, diminishing with each passing year, and in danger of being depleted within a short period of time. It is difficult to get far enough away from motorized river vessels no matter how far you walk into the forest. Nor is there a time (even at two in the morning) when the human-induced noises cease for more than a few minutes at a time.

Island Habitats

You will discover a wide variety of creature sound experiences on the various islands of the world that combine both desert and tropical rainforest environments. In Vanua Levu, one of the larger islands in the Fijian chain, there are several quiet locations to record. One particular site is a dry riparian habitat on a hill facing north about two kilometers from the ocean. At one time it was partially clearcut, which had an effect on the acoustic ambience. The dawn chorus, though, is lovely but lacking in both density and diversity, likely because of the sparse vegetation and erosion caused by human habitation that is evident everywhere. In the early dawn light you may hear the Fiji wood swallow, gray-backed white-eye, and several other species of birds. The silhouette of a huge bat gliding on the gentle currents offshore with a wingspan the size of a turkey vulture is a common sight. Just offshore, magnificent coral reef systems play host to many kinds of sea creatures whose acoustic signatures are accessible by hydrophone just below the surface. In the crystal-clear water, creatures are visible from above so they can be identified. Wave action is often light, so you can drop a hydrophone over the side of your boat to hear the sounds of the damselfish, three-spot dascyllus, parrot fish, wrasses, puffers, cardinals, fusiliers, goatfish, crustaceans, and butterfly fish—all playing their part in the reef biophony. The cracking, spitting, grunting, and percussive sounds all mix together in a staccato-like rhythm section that will bring a smile to your face.

Amazonia

Recording in the Amazon is always an adventure. In most cases while recording and listening in the field, you just might come upon something unusual. Remember, while there are constants, there's always a surprise lurking around the corner or under a log. Mindful listening will evoke a heightened sense of alertness. Whenever you walk through any jungle territory, day or night, especially where you have been informed that there might be poisonous snakes hidden under logs that can obstruct your path, you must dutifully shine a light in all likely spots, walk at a pace that allows you to pay extremely careful attention, and protect yourself and your gear from the unexpected. No matter how well trained or how proficient you think you are, being alone in such a place at such a time is guaranteed to raise your pulse rate significantly. Alertness is the key. Listen. Smell. Look. But mostly learn to listen.

In tropical rainforests you must be particularly mindful of the information every one of your senses offers: sight, smell, touch, and sound. Add to that any other sense you may have, and use them all.

(If it's your first time there, go with a knowledgeable guide.) The scent of a jaguar is especially characteristic. Most members of the feline family spray to mark their territory. In the case of *Panthera onca,* the scent it leaves is noticeable, even from a distance. Jaguars are among the strongest creatures in the animal kingdom, and one can drag a horse several times its weight many miles through the forest. Trying to record jaguars in their home territory is not recommended. I discovered this one night when I picked up the marking scent of one as it followed me down a trail well out of sight. No sooner had I set up my mic than the cat stepped up to the instrument and began to sniff, chuff, and growl. With luck, I lived to tell about it. Anytime you want to record a jaguar, I know a certain trail . . .

Indonesian Rainforests

Indonesian rainforests offer a wide variety of biomes, from wet to dry. The enhanced biophonic world that you will discover in places like Sumatra or Borneo will bring you into intimate contact with wildlife that you probably never thought possible. Gibbons, siamangs, orangutans, leaf monkeys, mustached babblers, white-rumped shamas, rhinoceros hornbills, Argus pheasants, insects, and frogs will all reveal themselves over time and you will get wonderful recordings.

While visiting Sumatra, you might even spot a rare clouded leopard as it stalks its way through the dense vegetation. Of all the leopard's finely distinguished rosette patterns and catlike features, its beautiful shape and grace as it glides elegantly by, nothing stands out more than its smallish, flat ears as they catch every nuance of sound. Every twig, each slight puff of air, even the sound of the blinking of your eyes will catch its attention. Although we think ourselves capable of overcoming most every obstacle in our limited nature, we humans are often brought up short by what we find in the relatively still vibrant forests of the world.

In Borneo, you will, of course, each have your own adventure. But the route we took to Camp Leakey by the riverboat we hired in Pangkalanbuun was notable. About thirty feet long and eight feet wide, with a shallow draft, the boat traveled at about five knots for a couple of days. These vessels are usually staffed with local families whose members serve as the crew, cooking and tending to the workings of the boat and the needs of a couple of guests, who pay for fuel, meals, a few square feet on top of the cargo to sleep, and a small number of extra necessities. Everyone on the small vessel sleeps together on a deck sheltered only by a roof completely open to the elements on all sides, except in severe weather, when curtains are lowered. We were only partially prepared for the journey. There's not much room, and not much of what my urban-sated sister would refer to as her "creature comforts." But for us, it was just fine.

Creature comforts were not our mission. Except for the noise of the badly tuned engine that knocked and sputtered, echoing off the riverbanks, shattering any semblance of connection with the forest ambience, it was a pleasant trip. Now and again, when the captain pulled to the shore, allowing us to stretch our badly cramped legs, we were able to catch moments of what we had come for—after our ears stopped ringing, that is, and if another such boat was not on the river when our crew chose to rest. Late on the second afternoon, we walked a mile or so inland from the water's edge and set up our mics in the forest. It is quiet in the jungle most afternoons before the daily weather cells pass by. Very still. No birds. Not even mosquitoes. Only a few lightly voiced cicadas, softer than one would imagine in the oppressive jungle heat of such a day. Their voices become so soft that they create a tension, suggesting something is about to happen. It gets quieter. Then quieter still. At first, we didn't notice the cumulous cloud formations partially hidden by the forest canopy, looming in the distance and heading toward us. But the creatures certainly did. The electricity in the air was palpable. By their silence, the creatures were telling us something we didn't quite understand; we western mortals hadn't yet relearned the subtleties of this atavistic narrative. Oblivious, we recorded stillness that gave us an unnerving feeling. Except for our breathing it was dead quiet, with not even the slightest movement registering on the recorder's level meter. So, of course, during the lull I made the mistake of cranking up the mic input volume trying to catch what little was there. The first colossal hit of lightning and thunder was so close and so loud that it shattered a nearby tree and nearly blew out the input to my recorder. Any closer and I would have been fried, because I forgot to take my earphones off—a no-no during a storm. Thinking I'd catch the next clap of thunder, I turned the input levels *way* down and detached the phones from the recorder. As soon as I did, the next thunder crack hit, this time farther away, but loud nevertheless. Luck was with us this time, and the event was caught on tape. Not thirty seconds later, we got another great ear-shattering boom that was near perfect and set the tone for the downpour to come.

The storm built to a stirring crescendo, the approaching rain generating a whoosh-like sound that was at first distant, then headed toward us so fast that it actually created a Doppler effect, rising in pitch and cutting through the forest with the impact of a fast-passing freight train. When the highest intensity reached our shelter, it virtually pinned the level meters on the recorder and we had to back off our already low-set levels to avoid overloading the input again. A terrific moment. Then, just as it had moved swiftly toward us, the storm receded, fading in loudness and dropping slightly in pitch (Doppler again), all of this drama occurring in just a few minutes. The thunder continued in the middle distance, and the lightning provided some memorable displays. The rain, which had decreased significantly, fairly dripped onto the forest vegetation, producing exquisitely fine poetic detail of sonic filigree. As the thunder rolls grew even more distant, insects began to reestablish their voices amid the rhythm of the intermittent post-storm drips. The insects continued for some time, firmly restoring their respective acoustic niches. Once these were in place, the first late-afternoon birds began to sing, followed by amphibians who joined in the chorus. In the relentless humidity and heat there was a feeling of release and freshness expressed by the biophony and the sweet scent of the forest. Reinvigorated and relaxed at the same time, we ambled back to the boat and headed upriver again toward our destination.

A couple of days later, we found ourselves tethered to the roots of a tree in a mangrove swamp. We were now in a dugout canoe made from a hollowed-out log that was none too stable as it sat very low in the water. The gunwales were only inches above the waterline, and we had to be very careful to stay centered to keep our equipment and ourselves from being swamped in the river's dark, tannin-colored water. We'd made this choice because we wanted to collect samples of the afternoon riverine soundscape, and the tree we tied our boat to provided such a spot. After a few minutes, we heard a succession of strange muddy splashes that appeared in our headphones. Anyone familiar with rainforest river life would know what the splashes meant. But we were new to this biome and didn't yet appreciate the rules. Soon enough, as we peered down into the darkened waters of the swamp, there were perhaps half a dozen four- or five-foot shadowy forms circling slowly just below the surface. We couldn't be sure of

the exact count. It was only then that we realized we were surrounded by crocodiles. I can be heard on the recording muttering,
"Maybe it's time to split." Indeed.

Costa Rica

In the heart of the San Juan River floodplain of the Osa Penin-
sula in Meso-America there is a mangrove swamp with a six-foot tidal
change. Set up your mics along the roadside timed for an evening
receding tide. As the water level drops, you'll hear popping and drip-
ping sounds coming from the tendrils of the mangrove vegetation.
If you shine your light on the source, you'll discover that the clamor
comes from families of crabs letting go of the tendrils and falling several feet into the outgoing tide water and mud below (because their
bodies need to stay moist). You'll also hear bats, mosquitoes, a fever-
ish mix of insects, tinamous, various types of tree frogs, and some
owls. Make certain that you are using the type of microphone that
won't fail from humidity. It hovers around 100 percent most of the
time there.

African Mountains

If you can get to Rwanda and the Virunga Mountains to record
the surviving mountain gorillas, it is worth the risk. When hiking to
find the gorillas each day, sometimes the trackers, researchers, and
tourists have to trudge three or four miles up and down steep moun-
tainous terrain between eight and twelve thousand feet, knee deep
in mud, vines, stinging nettles, and other secondary growth to finally
catch up with them. As I did, you'll need to learn to walk all over
again with a type of high-step especially peculiar to that kind of ter-

ritorial vegetation. To record the mountain gorillas, you will also need to secure access to the research groups through the requisite permits. Each (gorilla) group eats through a quarter mile of vegetation every day, finds a day nest to bed down in around midday, eats some more, and then finds a nesting site for the evening. By morning the gorillas are usually several miles from the previous day's site. Because they tend to cover a lot of territory, make sure that your equipment is light and made of components that are easy to set up, tear down, and pack. Also, make certain that when the gorillas approach out of curiosity to examine your equipment, easy targets such as mics, tripods, and cables are out of their reach. As they move you will frequently have to reposition yourself so you are able to catch whatever sporadic vocalizations are uttered. That could mean tearing down and setting up your equipment many times each hour. Flexibility in those surroundings is crucial.

With currently available technology, you could easily travel and record for a month or more in the field with not a lot of extra weight. Compact digital recorders are pocket-sized. The mic cable can be reduced to a single stereo line, and the headphones or ear buds are collapsible, light, and easily packed. Best of all, one set of lithium AA batteries can last about twenty-four hours in some devices. The whole contraption—recorder and all—weighs no more than a pound. Some recorders have built-in mics. Add to that a really good set of outboard mics and the necessary preamp and batteries to power them, along with a decent lightweight tripod, and you have a decent system. It will add a couple of pounds, but not much more. Best of all, a single 64-gigabyte compact flash card used in some recorders will cover you for more than sixty hours of stereo recording time at 44.1 kHz sampling and 24 bits per sample (half that at a sampling rate of 96 kHz).

In most cases, as with gorillas on the move, I would probably just stuff the whole shebang into a large pocket or backpack still plugged in, and move to the next site right along with them.

More Mountains

Mountain soundscape sites in general, depending on the level of difficulty in traversing the terrain, pose special problems of their own. Where there is wildlife, there are usually streams (noise) or wind. Where there are roads, there's usually a considerable amount of deforestation (fewer creatures). Where there are back-country trails, there's often either light or commercial aircraft (noise again). If those are not the issues, dirt bikers, distant chainsaws, domestic animals, and snowmobilers will be. These obstacles are particularly evident in North America. I don't care. I, like most of us, love the mountains and I just won't give up the chance of discovering great places to listen. The Nature Sounds Society, mentioned earlier, offers excellent introductory nature-sound field programs and workshops during the year. Each June, around the time of the solstice, there is usually a field workshop located at the San Francisco State University research site near Yuba Pass, just north of Truckee in the Sierra Nevada—which is John Muir territory. One of the better and more accessible introductory programs offered in the world of natural sound, this annual weekend event takes beginning listeners and recordists to the coniferous forests of Yuba Pass, down to a watershed in Sierra Valley and other nearby locations, where dawn and evening choruses are featured. Also, the society is equally strong on the issue of species-specific creatures and covers many recording philosophies and techniques. You need to get yourselves there. But once at the station, tent sites, hearty food, well-versed mentors, informative presenters, and a wide range of recordists will help make things easy for you. The entire fact-loaded and eventful weekend can be had for a bit over two hundred dollars, and anyone can join (http://www .naturesounds.org/announcements/index.html).

Yuba Pass

Here is a good example of what you can find at the Nature Sounds Society program. Early one morning in 1988, while scheduled to give a talk at their workshop, I happened to venture off alone to a place off the Yuba Pass ridgeline called Lincoln Meadow. It is a wide green meadow about two-thirds of a mile (one kilometer) long and a quarter mile (four hundred meters) wide, replete with wildflowers, fledging birds, and a clear trout stream stretching from the southern end at the edge of the woods diagonally to the northernmost point. Even though it may be a paragon in my mind and folks might look at me with hooded eyes as I attempted to describe in words its fragile beauty, it's what Edward Abbey describes as "beyond the ordinary limits of human experience." At one point it was something not even a camera could capture. That June, I managed to record on tape one of those moments rife with all of its mystery and charm intact.

A year later, when I returned, selective logging had taken place at the northwestern end, a process, the logging company had assured everyone, that would have no environmental impact on the site. Yet the biophonies that had once made Lincoln Meadow a beguiling place no longer existed. What remained was, at the time, off-limits, according to the lumber-company sign postings. For one thing, enough of the primary forest at the southern end had been cleared away that it left the stream silted and cloudy as it ran downhill to the north. Once again, I recorded so that I had a sample of what it sounded like before and after—one of the few places that this comparison has actually been done. The contrast can be heard on our web site, at www.wildsanctuary.com.[3] I have revisited Lincoln Meadow fifteen times in the past twenty-six years and found that much of the meadow and the stream *look* quite healthy, at least from the perspective of the eye or a camera. But aside from the effects of the wind and the gentle stream, the dawn chorus of birdsong has never recovered its vitality. Certainly the recordings I have on tape from before the selective logging show that this was an environment containing much more biophonic activity than it does now. The example clearly demonstrates that we need lots more before-and-after examples, and I encourage those of you who love natural soundscapes to begin collecting those types of biophonies.

Some think that the fall, between mid-September and early October, is particularly quiet. Perhaps, in some parts of the country. But if you want an exciting recording experience at that time of year, head out to Yellowstone National Park to hear the elk bugle. Locate yourself at the northeastern end of the Lamar Valley, where the Druid pack of wolves is easy to spot. It is an area that tends to be more lightly traveled and therefore generates a bit less noise than other areas of the park. From the Pebble Creek campsite, hike away from the stream up the hill to the northwest away from the main trail until you come to a series of open meadows. Hide yourself in the tree line upwind and along the eastern forest edge. Set up your recording system and wait. Within a short time you should hear some bugling. Just pray that the elk won't catch your scent (a bit like hoping the sun won't rise in the east). Elk have learned about predators over time; never mind that you are armed only with recorders. The introduction of the wolves has raised their levels of alertness even higher than in the past, and they are easily spooked. Dawn is best, but they bugle at dusk and other times of day as well. Since they often pass through that area, you may be lucky enough to get bugling up close and personal. It takes patience, however, and you might need to plant yourselves there over the course of several days to capture just the right sound.

Along the edge habitats of the meadows, you can also record the fall voices of ravens, grouse, a merlin, geese, downy woodpeckers, larks, juncos, house sparrows, cedar waxwings, and kingbirds. Yellowstone is a thousand miles from our home, but I'd make the trip once a week if I had the money for gas.

Teton and Yellowstone

On your way to or from Yellowstone, also stop in the Tetons to check for elk—especially during the fall rut. Heading north out of Jackson past the airport, you'll come to a road leading to Moose and the entrance to Grand Teton National Park. Turn west there and follow your map to White Grass Meadows to hear the bugling at dusk. Grand Teton is the only national park with a full-service jet-sanctioned airport, located right in the middle of the valley—so there's a *lot* of noise. When a 737 or a private jet takes off—depending on prevailing winds—it can be heard ten miles away. (This, incidentally, is the new fly-in home of many movie stars—some of them claiming to be environmentalists who moved to Jackson to avoid the noise and urbanization of Aspen, Vail, and L.A. During high seasons, as many as twenty-two departures and landings per hour are possible.) In addition, White Grass Meadows also comes with some stream noise. So, while this is not a particularly great place to record, it is a fine site where you can hear and observe the elk. During one of the aircraft departure lulls, it turned out to be the only place where I've been able to record the sound of snow falling.

Never give up your search for decent places to record. On a dirt road leading to the east, about eighteen miles north of Moose junction off Highway 191, you should find "FR 30310" on many forest service or detailed contour maps. Follow this around to the north (stay to the left where the roads fork) and east about five miles and you'll come to a watershed with marshes, a small pond (the water level depends on the previous winter's precipitation), and some edge habitat that has everything you could dream of, including frogs, birds, insects, mammals, *and* it's in a relative noise-shadow of most of the Jackson Hole valley, including the airport. We recorded over several days, hearing few aircraft and very light auto traffic on the dirt road leading to the site or from the main highway in the valley below (Highway 191). You can record both freshwater marine and terrestrial biomes there and discover some terrific wildlife soundscapes including elk. In addition, a newly released pack of wolves is reported to be in the vicinity that you might hear and be able to record.

Marine Ecosystems

You'd think as you stand on the seashore looking out at the waves that they'd be easy to record. They're certainly accessible and easy to hear and listen to. All-pervasive. All-encompassing. The sound, the salt air, the moisture on your skin, all suggest that ocean waves at the shore would be an effortless target. One of my biggest surprises in the field of recording was my continued inability to capture on tape what I experienced with my ears. Every time I went to the shore to record, I would place a mic where I thought I was hearing the best iteration of ocean waves. And each time I returned to my studio and played back the tapes, they failed to evoke a sense of what I had heard and imagined. In fact, the sound was usually so thin and flat, so lacking in presence or dynamic, at first I thought it was a bad choice of my mic system.

I was younger then, and believed fully in the divinity of technology coupled with the efficacy of our large brain. So I invested in more and more elaborate and expensive mics (all recommended by professional colleagues), and went often to the shore to capture the elusive ocean signatures. I returned to the studio only to be disappointed again and again. Turns out that the problem was not with the microphones. It was with *me* and the way I had been taught to listen. Basically, as I said previously, I was conditioned to hear what I was looking at. When I looked directly at waves breaking in the distance, I heard the deep thunderous low-frequency roar as the waves curled and pounded into the surf. When I looked near-field at the waves breaking closer to shore, I heard more detail—a larger sense of water movement. And when, at last, I would see the lip of the waves moving up the rake of the beach with the leading edge stopping at my feet, I distinctly heard the tiny bubbles bursting as water met sand. It was only when I shut my eyes, eliminating the visual distraction, that my mind translated the sound into something approaching the compelling and resonant voice I had come to the beach to hear, after all. The solution, given the limitations of all the mics I had chosen, was to record waves from different perspectives and combine them all later in a mix that aids the ear to pick up the breadth and depth of the whole acoustic field.

This insight, which took ten years of trial and error to achieve, led me to rethink what I had been neglecting with my mics and recorders. The truth is that, no matter what the manufacturers' claims or how expensive your equipment turns out to be, all of these tools are only partially adequate to the task. Each component has been de-signed for a special limited purpose based on certain criteria that designers incorporate into their products. So every choice is a com-promise.

To the untrained ear, most insect, frog, or bird choruses sound similar at first. And, yes, even waves at the ocean shore. However, one of the fascinating things about recording is its revelation that ocean waves may, indeed, sound different from place to place. For one thing there's the ambient sound of occasional shore birds that triggers a sense of locale. Different beaches, different secondary and tertiary dune grasses, different onshore sites and climate, and the subtle mixes of all those components provide the necessary clues. In addition, the rake of the beach affects wave action—like periodicity and force—the contrasts of which register pretty clearly on tape. Some beaches have very active and violent action. Others sound more gentle. The rhythm of the waves also differs from beach to beach, high tide to low, stormy to calm conditions, and season to season. In fact it is likely that each site has its own very distinctive range of signatures and performances. It is also possible that creatures may be partially drawn to the special geophony of particular coastal sites—that is, the man-ner in which the geographical features of a location contribute to the performance of their voices.

In the same way ocean coastal shorelines sound different to my ear, so do inland freshwater lakes, for much the same reasons. With freshwater habitats, the wave movement tends to be more gentle on average, with more of a quick rhythmic lapping staccato sound. Fresh water is less dense.

I've recorded beaches from the tip of Latin America, in Africa, Madagascar, the Azores, New Zealand, Australia, Fiji, and the west coast of North America from Baja California to Alaska, including large freshwater lakes. When I rack them up to audition, comparing them side by side, they all sound different, which is likely a factor of the surrounding landscape, as well as how I position my mics although I'm pretty careful to be consistent with my setups. While weather and other conditions vary all over the place, most of these were recorded in much the same manner with comparable equipment. Although, to be fair, when these samples were recorded, they weren't done with the idea of comparisons in mind. I wasn't specifically *listening* for sites that would match. Since none of them do, it's my guess that if you've heard one beach, you've (only) heard the unique geophony of one beach.

Plains

Described to some extent in Chapter 4, wind is a constant challenge when trying to record creatures and sounds of the world's remaining grasslands. Yet it's a grand effect to capture, by itself, in a recording. Three primary effects come immediately to mind: wind through the trees, wind in the grasses, and pitched wind (wind that changes tone). For wind in the trees, find some aspens (called "quakies" in the American West). They really *do* quake—gently. When you stand under a young aspen, one with shimmering leaf-filled branches not more than eight feet above the ground, you might get a recording that will *sound* like leaves blowing in the wind. Mostly, though, what you will get is a recording that sounds more like close-up surf, or rain, or something not-quite-wind- or leaf-like. My best aspen recordings were made on Trail Creek Road (FR 208) heading east out of Ketchum, Idaho. At the top of the ridge in the Challis National Forest there are a number of spots just off the road where one can record for short periods (intermittent traffic). To get the leaf sound,

I parked the car under the tree, using the car's body to shelter the mics from the very strong gusts blowing at the top of the ridge. This setup is not ideal, but the results sound just like what you would imagine wind in the trees to be. In your mix, by changing levels from low to high, you can give the impression of everything from light breezes to high, gale-force blows.

Normally, with most recordings, it's really quite difficult to distinguish wind in the trees from wind in grasses. But there is a difference. When grasses are recorded properly, they sound different—much closer to the components of rain than well-recorded shafts of vegetation. That's because when the leaves of grass hit each other in the wind, the sound is more a result of friction and release than percussion. Contact between blades tends to be very light and sounds high pitched. If you can get your mics in position to capture the illusion, you've succeeded. Experiment with different mics to see which ones provide the impression you desire. For one thing, your mics will need to be kept away from the direct force of the wind. That means getting them very close to or directly on the ground. Lavaliere (lav) mics are probably best for this purpose. If you're using omnidirectional lav mics, you might try attaching them to a particularly strong leaf of grass or the small branch of a nearby low-lying bush. From my experience, however, ground level is better. That way, if all conditions conspire in your favor, you will get a good recording. Monitor the sound through your headphones with your eyes closed, though. If you have your mics positioned right and they are picking up wind effect blowing through the grass along with the light "clicks" of grass blades hitting and rubbing against each other, you're good. If it sounds even vaguely like rain, it will sound more like rain when you get home without the visual cues to confirm the sources of the signal. You may have traveled a long way to get this sound, so work on the illusion until it is just right and evokes the mental image you wish to convey. Keep in mind that some lavaliere mics—especially the less expensive models—tend to be a bit noisy, but the loud signal of the wind through the blades of grass should mitigate that problem.

The pitched sound of whistling wind is one of my favorite effects. It is also difficult to find, isolate, and record. The best example I found was by walking an old barbed wire fence line on a windy spring day in the panhandle of New Mexico, although I'm sure a barbed wire fence in Maine, Montana, Saskatchewan, Alabama, South Dakota, or the Pampas of Argentina would do just as well. Twists in the taut wire nearest to the ground tend to alter the pitch of the wind higher or lower as a result of its changing velocity. Set your mics directly on the ground and record. You might also be able to do the same thing by just cracking a window open in your house on a particularly windy night and setting the mics back a foot or so from the opening. It is not necessary to use lavaliere mics for this one. Nearly any type will do. The effect can be surprisingly evocative (as long as you live in a relatively quiet neighborhood).

As for the effects of wind, I am reminded of an event that became one of my most important recording and music lessons. On a cold October morning many years ago, while working with the Nez Percé tribe on their Idaho reservation, an elder took me to a sacred tribal spot in northeastern Oregon, where I was encouraged to sit by the side of a stream and consider the ways in which music might have been revealed to his ancestors. For a long while I remained still and heard nothing. Then, as the late morning wind began to blow down the length of the canyon, I heard what sounded like a giant pipe organ but had no idea what caused it. When Angus Wilson, the elder, pointed out that certain reeds by the stream's edge had been broken at different lengths by the force of the wind and were whistling at different pitches, I understood immediately how his descendants were bound to create instruments like the reed flute and make music inspired by the breath of the forest.

Recording the Unseen

Another unexpected discovery for me was the first time I heard insect larvae in a pool of water by the curb outside my house. The pool was formed by a spring rainstorm. I was just experimenting with the hydrophone and decided to drop it into the puddle. It was alive with sounds I later realized were caused by water boatmen, small insects that thrive on decaying wood and other underwater debris. Along with the water boatmen there were other sounds that I couldn't identify, but which later turned out to be insect larvae. It's worth obtaining some special gear to help hear these wonders. Our ears were meant to hear perfectly in air, but not in water. Marine sounds can be as astounding and worth hearing as those found on land.

In the insect world, ants are among the most extraordinary creatures to capture sound from. Usually we cannot hear them with our ears alone (unless, of course, you like the idea of fire ants crawling along your Eustachian tube). But we certainly can hear some species with the help of small, inexpensive lavaliere microphones laid over the top of the main entrance to their underground homes. I defy folks to keep a straight face when they hear the delightful voices of these creatures for the first time. Our ears were meant to hear sounds at some low levels, but not as subtle as some of the smaller creatures can produce. One group of researchers in the United Kingdom has even managed to record the sound of viruses.[4]

Arctic Habitats

If you feel really ambitious, try the Yukon Delta and the Arctic National Wildlife Refuge. The truly remote and wild locations of the world require serious planning and substantial resources to get to, not to mention having your level of security challenged by putting yourself in a situation where you're completely alone and out of touch with the comfort zone you've left behind for long uncertain periods. But, to my mind, these types of trips are worth every ambiguity, every risk. All of the other recording sites mentioned above are easy to get into and out of. While, to some, those places might seem exotic enough, there is still some measure of support (such as food and accommodations or transportation at some basic level) nearby. In the Yukon Delta and the Arctic National Wildlife Refuge, however, you must be completely self-sufficient in every way possible. After you're flown in and dropped off, there's no way to easily or reliably call for a flight to take you out on a moment's notice—often because bad weather is a factor, but also because unless the pickup time is scheduled in advance, you will likely be out of radio range, nowhere near a cell tower or Internet connection—that is if you're remote enough. But these are precisely the places I like to visit and record most of all, if for no other reason than the fact that they deliver the longest periods of time without human noise or distraction. It is where I feel most alive and alert.

At Yukon Delta National Wildlife Refuge, our campsite, at the eastern base of the Askinuk Mountains, was located about 130 air miles northwest of Bethel, Alaska. I chose that spot in particular because in the western Alaskan tundra, I could record a wide variety of both inland and shore birds, as well as (hopefully) a few mammals. For two weeks, my wife, Katherine, and I took with us a three-week supply of food in bear-proof containers, a Coleman stove (since we could not rely on any wood for fires), the usual warm clothing and a tent, a good supply of batteries to power the equipment, pepper spray and a shotgun to dissuade predators, and fishing tackle. (Note: It is highly inadvisable to venture any place where you might need a firearm without first knowing how to use it absolutely safely and effectively and feeling completely comfortable with the device in your hands.)

In ten days on the ground we only heard one jet aircraft high overhead, probably bound for Asia or Russia. In early June, when we went, it was light enough to read for all but one or two hours in any twenty-four-hour cycle, because we were just a few degrees south of the Arctic Circle. This meant I could record around the clock and also that there was no distinctive dawn, dusk, or nighttime chorus as in lower, more temperate, latitudes. And, luckily for us, the weather was good for almost the entire time we were on the ground. Speaking of ground, since there are no trees and only a few examples of low scrub vegetation, most of the nests were at ground level. We had to be quite careful where we stepped to avoid disturbing any of the eggs or nesting birds. In the delta, you'll discover a wonderful mix of birds including the savanna sparrow, fox sparrow, white-crowned sparrow, dark-eyed junco, Wilson's warbler, orange-crowned warbler, yellow wagtail, hoary redpoll, ruby-crowned kinglet, wheatear, snipe, long-tailed jaeger, merganser, common whistling swan, grebes, Arctic tern, scaup, glaucous gull, rock ptarmigan, goshawk, Arctic loon, northern pintail (duck), and Canada geese. We saw an Arctic fox but it never vocalized so that I could record it. Although there was some variation of biophonic density and diversity over the course of a twenty-four-hour cycle, those dynamic changes never occurred at distinct times. Nevertheless, the biophonies were rich and almost always present.[5]

Once you've honed your field techniques to a workable model and feel confident recording in the field under a range of conditions, here's a more challenging adventure: Pull together one or more teams of recordists to cover different ecoregions within a large geographical territory. The Arctic National Wildlife Refuge, located in the northeastern quadrant of the state of Alaska, is more than thirty thousand square miles in size. As you can imagine, an area that large includes many ecosystem types, ranging from the coastal north slope along the Beaufort Sea, the Brooks Range of mountains cutting diagonally across the refuge to the south, and even the westernmost part of the boreal forest that stretches from the Canadian Maritimes all the way across to Alaska and into parts of the refuge. The acoustic surface of this astounding place has barely been explored by sound recordists. In 2005, I discovered that the biophonies there had never been recorded under any circumstances, and also that a couple of Alaskan senators had been promoting oil drilling in the refuge by assuring their colleagues that there was nothing living there. In addition to these factors, the effects of global warming were already being noted in Alaska, so I decided to initiate a mission titled *The Arctic Soundscape Project,* designed to address our lack of knowledge and let whatever we found enjoy the light of transparency. With generous support from the U.S. Fish and Wildlife Service (especially Roger Kaye), Google, Harvard University, Stanford University, Skywalker Sound (a division of LucasFilm), the Animal Welfare Institute, University of Utah (Marriott Library), the Calgary Zoo, Patagonia clothing company, the Maine Community Foundation, and donations from many individuals in the community where we live, we managed to raise the necessary funding to take three teams to different sites in the refuge in early June 2006.

One site, with Dr. Kevin Colver, was located at the Beaufort Lagoon, just a few miles west of the Canadian border, at the water's edge of the Beaufort Sea where there were a great many migrating shore birds. Colver was assisted by Robert Thompson, a very well respected Inupiat guide for *National Geographic* from Kaktovik. Martyn Stewart settled in about seventy miles to the south at a place called Sunset Pass, on the north slope in the foothills of the Brooks Range. He was aided by another guide, Andy Keller. I camped south of the Brooks Range at an abandoned hunting camp called Timber Lake, along with the guide Frank Keim and associate Bob Moore from Maine. As it happened, we had earlier mapped out twenty-one sites as possible destinations, but by the time we had to make final decisions in early June, the tundra surface at eighteen of those sites was already too soft and compromised to support the landings of even light aircraft. Spring had occurred several weeks earlier than normal that year.

Sticking to a strict recording protocol (with similar equipment, times scheduled to record, and calibrations determined in advance so that the study could be repeated to note similarities and changes because of changing climate conditions), between us we managed to capture biophonies that included more than a hundred species of birds, many different kinds of mammals, and even a few insects. Most notable was the fact that American robins had already migrated well north into the refuge because of the warming climate. The bird is rarely seen that far north, and several of the Native American enclaves in and around the refuge didn't even have a name for it because it was so new and uncommon to them. The end result of the project was that we now have a significant baseline collection of material recorded in those remote ecoregions available for future research and enjoyment. Despite its dismissal by some politicians not known for their scientific literacy, the refuge is, indeed, quite resonant with wild-life sound.[6]

> When the animals come to us,
> asking for our help,
> will we know what they are saying?
>
> When the plants speak to us
> in their delicate, beautiful language,
> will we be able to answer them?
>
> When the planet herself
> sings to us in our dreams,
> will we be able to wake ourselves, and act?
> —*Gary Lawless, "When the Animals Come to Us"*

Afterword

Unlike most descriptions of the natural world, this book has not sought to answer any profound questions—only to raise them, by introducing you to the limitless possibilities inherent in the budding field of soundscape ecology and to open up the probability of new and more cogent observations and contributions you will make to this quickly expanding field. Natural sound is a form of narrative poetry. It is only through our close acoustic observations that we begin to sense the enormous mysteries of a world of life we now need to decipher. What we once thought of as disparate elements and chaotic noise really is a cohesive statement of the living environment, what Jane Hirshfield, author of *Ten Windows,* refers to as "generative recombination," the recognition and discernment of vital patterns. Listening to and recording the exquisite narratives expressed through the lens of our soundscape universe helps us come to terms with the possibility that we might never achieve more than a tiny glimpse of the fabric's shapes and colors. But with good microphones, a decent set of ears, and the will to listen more closely, perhaps we will find a measure of intimacy and consolation in those precious voices after all, along with the will to preserve them, whatever the cost.

Binaural Recording Issues

by Lang Elliott

If you record using a binaural-type setup (using two omnidirectional mics placed at a comparable distance to the space between your ears and mounted in a headlike holder), then you are theoretically preserving the "spatial cues" that our brains use to determine the whereabouts of sounds in natural situations. These include signal time arrival differences at each ear, intensity differences between ears due to the head-shadowing effect, and phase differences depending on the frequency, plus other subtle stuff like head size, and shape, and the size and shape of the pinnae.

In order to feed these cues back to the brain on playback, it is critical that a clean left mic signal is channeled to the left ear and a clean right mic signal reaches the right ear. What you don't want is for the left ear to hear the right signal and vice versa, because such "crosstalk" will cancel out the spatial cues that are so valuable to us when trying to determine the source of a particular sound within a soundscape.

Headphone listening, to some extent, meets these criteria, but has some apparent weaknesses. The main weakness is that, due to the physical closeness of the headphone speaker elements to the ears, many of the resulting sounds appear to come from inside your head, rather than "out in a spatial soundscape" where they belong. This is especially a problem with sounds originating front and center; these sounds appear largely to be in your head when using headphones, even when the recording was made using high-quality binaural mic'ing techniques.

Conventional "stereo" speaker playback completely destroys spatial cues because of crosstalk (because our right ear hears the left speaker and the left ear hears the right). Thus, even if the recording is rich in spatial cues, it is degraded by the stereo playback technique itself. The result is that we end up having to rely on a very unnatural way to determine the whereabouts of the sound sources, based primarily on intensity differences between the two speakers. A sound that is louder in the right speaker will appear to come from that direction, and vice versa. Sounds appear to come from the center when they are of equal loudness in both speakers. This explains the familiar "phantom center" in stereo playback. Conventional stereo is a system full of acoustic compromises that tends to compress and distort spaciousness and localization, though it admittedly sounds good if one has never heard a better alternative. It is what we're used to.

One can reduce or eliminate the crosstalk problem in several ways. An easy, but awkward, solution is to use a barrier. It goes like this: set two speakers together and insert a physical barrier between them, such as a piece of plywood three or four feet long extending out toward the listener. Then, sit at the end of the barrier with your nose tight to the plywood and listen to a binaural nature recording. Suddenly, you will hear sounds extending out in an arc approaching 150 degrees, far wider than a stereo replication, and incredibly dimensional and realistic. It is called three-dimensional sound because of the marvelous sense of depth produced. It is referred to as "virtual" 3-D because the sounds aren't really coming from where you hear them. What's happening is that our brains are receiving the natural spatial cues in the binaural recording and automatically placing the sounds where they're supposed to be.

Now there are "crosstalk canceling" solutions that allow a listener to remove the barrier and still get the same effect, as long as the listener sits along the axis between the speakers at an optimal distance. One such system, the UltraQ, accomplishes this using proprietary analog circuitry. Other, more advanced solutions involve digital signal processing, or DSP, which enables us to process recordings before playing them back, and perhaps, even encode the binaural signal with the anti-crosstalk format.

Some crosstalk-canceling solutions work best with the speakers placed apart, either at the conventional sixty-degree triangle position (meaning that the listener forms the apex of an equaliteral triangle with speakers located in front), or else with the speakers a little closer together. A couple of the more recent and advanced DSP solutions work optimally if the speakers are placed much closer together, at a fifteen to twenty degree angle with respect to the listener.

Further Resources

Sounds

Sound examples indicated in the book by ⌇⌇ are available at yalebooks .com/wildsoundscapes

Guide Books

D. J. Borror, *Field Guide to Insects—America North of Mexico* (Boston: Houghton Mifflin, 1998)

H. G. Cogger, *Encyclopedia of Reptiles and Amphibians* (New York: Academic Press, 1998)

Lang Elliot, *Music of the Birds: A Celebration of Bird Song,* book and CD (Boston: Houghton Mifflin Press, 1999)

E. Lieske and R. Myers, *Coral Reef Fishes* (Princeton, N.J.: Princeton University Press, 1996)

L. J. Milne, *National Audubon Society Field Guide to North American Insects and Spiders,* 2nd edition (New York: DK Publishing, 2000)

L. Mound, *Eyewitness: Insect* (New York: DK Publishing, 2000)

J. R. Paxton, *Encyclopedia of Fishes,* 2nd edition (New York: Academic Press, 1998)

Organizations

British Library of Wildlife Sounds (http://www.bl.uk/collections/sound archive/wild.html)

Cornell University, Library of Natural Sounds (http://birds.cornell.edu /LNS)

NatureRecordists (naturerecordists@yahoogroups.com)

An Informational Chat Format for Field Recording and Technology at All Levels of Interest

Nature Sounds Society, 290 Napoleon St., Studio E, San Francisco, Calif. 94124 (http://www.naturesounds.org)

Programs and Introductory Field Workshops

Noise Pollution Clearinghouse: Les Blomberg, P.O. Box 1137, Montpelier, Vt. 05601-1137, Tel.: 888-200-8332 (http://www.nonoise.org)

Quiet Down America (http://www.quietdownamerica.com)

Wild Sanctuary (http://www.wildsanctuary.com)

World Forum for Acoustic Ecology (http://www.wfae.net)

British Library of Wildlife Sounds (http://www.bl.uk/collections/sound archive/wild.html)

International Society of Ecoacoustics (ISE) (https://sites.google.com/site /ecoacousticssociety/about)

Macaulay Library of Bird Sound, Cornell University Library of Natural Sounds (http://www.birds.cornell.edu/page.aspx?pid=1676)

NatureRecordists: An international chat format for field recording and related technologies at all levels of interest (naturerecordists@yahoogroups .com)

Soundscape Outfitters and Guides

Spirit Walker Expeditions, Gustavus, Alaska, 1-800-529-2537 (www .seakayakalaska.com), specializing in southeastern Alaska

On Safari International, Harare, Zimbabwe (osi@ecoweb.co.zw or Solomon@mweb.co.zw [Derek Solomon]), specializing in south, south-central, and east African sound safaris (http://www.kuyimba.com /safarimain.html), soundscape safari adventures hosted by Derek & Sarah Solomon

Discography
Bernie Krause

http://wildstore.wildsanctuary.com

A Wild Christmas, with Phil Aaberg (Wild Sanctuary, 1998)

African Adventures (Wild Sanctuary, 1998)

All Good Men, with Paul Beaver (Warner Brothers, 1973)

Alpine Meadow (Wild Sanctuary, 2002)

Amazon Days, Amazon Nights (Wild Sanctuary, 1998)

Borneo: Paradise in Kalimantan (Wild Sanctuary, 1998)

Citadels of Mystery (Takoma/Mobile Fidelity, 1979)

Dawn at Trout Lake (Wild Sanctuary, 1998)

Desert Solitudes, with Ruth Happel (Wild Sanctuary, 1994)

Discover the Wonder, grades 3–6 (Scott Foresman, 1992)

Distant Thunder (Nature Company, 1988)

Equator (Nature Company, 1986)

Gandharva, with Paul Beaver (Warner Brothers, 1971)

Gentle Ocean (Nature Company, 1988)

Gorilla (Nature Company, 1989)

Gorillas in the Mix (Rykodisc, 1988)

Mata Atlantica, Atlantic Rainforest, with Ruth Happel (Wild Sanctuary, 1994)

Meridian, with Philip Aaberg (Nature Company, 1990)

Midsummer Nights, with Ruth Happel (Wild Sanctuary, 1998)

Morning Song Birds (Nature Company, 1988)

Mountain Stream (Nature Company, 1988)

Music of Nez Perce (Wild Sanctuary, 1991)

Natural Voices/African Song Cycle (Wild Sanctuary, 1990)

Nature (Nature Company, 1987)

Nature's Lullabies, Wee Creatures, ages 1–3

Nez Perce Stories (Wild Sanctuary, 1991)

Nonesuch Guide to Electronic Music (Nonesuch, 1968)

Ocean, Rain & Stream (3 titles, Wild Sanctuary, 1994)

Ocean Dreams (Wild Sanctuary, 1998)

Ocean Odyssey, with Rodney Franklin (Wild Sanctuary, 1998)

Ocean Wonders (Wild Sanctuary, 1998)

Ragnarok, with Paul Beaver (Limelite, 1969)

Rainforest Dreams, with Rodney Franklin (Wild Sanctuary, 1998)

Revised Nonesuch Guide to Electronic Music (Nonesuch, 1979)

Rhythms of Africa, with Rodney Franklin (Wild Sanctuary, 1998)

Sounds of a Summer's Evening (Nature Company, 1988)

Tropical Rainforest (Nature Company, 1989)

Tropical Thunder (Wild Sanctuary, 1991)

Tundra in Spring (Wild Sanctuary, 2002)

Whales, Wolves & Eagles of Glacier Bay (Wild Sanctuary, 1998)

Wild Times at the Waterhole (Wild Sanctuary, 1991)

Woodland Journey (Wild Sanctuary, 1990)

Others

Antarctica, Doug Quin* (Wild Sanctuary, 1998)

Bayaka: The Extraordinary Music of the BaBenzele Pygmies, Louis Sarno* (Ellipses Arts, 1996)

Drums Across the Tundra, Chuna McIntyre (Wild Sanctuary, 1992)

Loons of Echo Pond, Ruth Happel* (Wild Sanctuary, 1998)

Madagascar: Gardens of Eden, Doug Quin* (Wild Sanctuary, 1998)

* Bernie Krause, Executive Producer

Videos

Bernie Krause, TED Global talk, presented June 2013, Edinburgh, Scotland (http://www.ted.com/talks/bernie_krause_the_voice_of_the_natural_world.html)

Glossary

acoustic   pertaining to the physics of sound.

acoustic ecology   the study of how sound in given environments affects humans and non-humans alike. A term brought into the lexicon by R. Murray Schafer and Barry Truax from Simon Fraser University in Vancouver, British Columbia, in the late 1970s.

acoustic signature   a characteristic sound pattern, call, or vocalization produced by any living organism.

ambient sound   surrounding, encircling, as in sounds that seem to permeate and envelop entire ecoregions.

amplitude   in acoustics, a signal level measured in decibels.

analog   in the field of audio recording, it refers to the transformation of audio signals into electromagnetic impulses, which are then transmitted to and stored on media such as audiotape made up of a mylar backing coated with particles of oxide (the size of smoke molecules) and held together by an adhesive process. As the tape moves past the electromagnetic heads of the recorder, the oxide is reconfigured into patterns corresponding to the audio input. These patterns can later be read on playback as an audio signal.

anthropophony   the final component of the soundscape that includes two subclasses of human-generated sound. The first of these subclasses is controlled sound, including music, theater, and language. The second of these subclasses is incoherent or chaotic sound, often referred to as noise.

anthroposphere   that part of the environment that is made or modified by humans for use in human activities and human habitats.

audio spectrum the range of sounds, from lowest to highest, that an organism can detect.

binaural type of recording system that attempts to reproduce in playback the illusion of sound as we typically hear it, coming from all perspectives (up, down, all-around).

bioacoustician one who studies the sounds produced by living organisms or the broader field of soundscape ecology.

bioacoustic boundaries refers to amoeba-shaped territories that particular creatures vocalize in as part of mating, feeding, conflict, and other rituals; a territory defined by its bioacoustic margins.

bioacoustics study of the sounds produced by living organisms.

biome a large community of plants and animals that occupies a distinct region. Terrestrial biomes, typically defined by their climate and dominant vegetation, include grassland, tundra, desert, tropical rainforest, and deciduous and coniferous forests. Marine communities include kelp forests along coastal (littoral) ranges, coral reefs, and deep ocean (pelagic) ecoregions.

biophony the collective sound that whole groups of living organisms produce in a given ecosystem; the second of three components of the soundscape.

brown noise usually refers to a power density that decreases 6 dB per octave as the frequency increases.

cacophony a din of noise created by unrelated sound.

cans slang or jargon for headphones.

cardioid heart-shaped microphone pickup pattern.

DAT digital audiotape, a recording technology common from the late 1980s until the early 2000s.

decibel (dB) the common practical unit for the logarithmic expression of ratios of loudness, power, voltage, current, etc.

distortion occurs when the normal shape of the audio wave form is altered in a manner that it no longer conveys the information cohesively. In professional terms, this occurs when the amplitude of a signal exceeds the ability of the technology to read or record it. That occurrence is referred to as clipping. Another type of distortion is introduced by the inability of digital equipment to read very high frequency signals. This type is called aliasing. And yet another is introduced by the inability of a microphone to read and capture certain complex signals that contain unrelated harmonic content.

echo the discernible repetition of a sound in either an indoor or an outdoor site.

echolocation the location of objects by reflected sound waves in either indoor or outdoor habitats.

ecotone a transitional zone between types of habitats.

equalizer a device that can increase signal strength in selected portions of the audible spectrum in a recording.

filter a device for attenuating selected portions of the audible spectrum.

frequency the number of complete cycles of a periodic signal occurring in a given time span. The unit in general use is designated in hertz (Hz), where 1 Hz is equal to one cycle per second.

geophony the original source of sound on earth, made up of nonbiological natural sounds such as the effect of water in marine environments, wind in the trees, thunder, rain, earthquakes, avalanches; the first of three elements in the soundscape.

hertz (Hz) the standard measurement of sound wave frequency; 1 Hz is equal to one cycle per second.

hydrophone an underwater microphone.

kopje (also koppie) a granite outcropping found in southern Africa: the term derives a diminutive of the Dutch word *kop,* or "head."

infrasound usually referred to as those sounds lower in frequency than the human capacity to detect (less than 20 Hz).

lek a patch of ground used for communal display during breeding season by the males of certain birds and mammals, especially the greater sage grouse.

loudness refers to the perceived intensity of sound. Loudness is not always a measure of sound pressure level and can be sensed as being loud by virtue of its particular texture or timbre.

M-S mid-side, a two-channel microphone system consisting of two different types of mics. One is a type of cardioid pattern, the second is a figure-eight pattern. The resultant recording provides numerous options for archiving and mixing. M-S decoding is required to transform M-S recordings into a robust left/right stereo image.

microphone a device that transforms vibrations transmitted through the air into corresponding electrical signals.

mix any choice an artist makes when combining two or more separate audio elements to produce the final expression of a recording.

monaural a single-channel recording designed for listening to one output source.

monophonic a class of recorded sound originating from a single media track.

noise for the purpose of this document, unwanted sound: any sound that impairs accurate transmission of useful and helpful acoustic information.

noise pollution the concept that an environment can be negatively affected by unwanted sound.

octave a difference in frequency (Hz) of either double or half in relation to a primary tone. In a Western diatonic music scale, this is the eighth tone in the musical scale higher or lower from a fundamental pitch.

optical sound track a method of producing sound on film by a type of narrow barcode-like stripe running along one side of the film strip. A beam of light is projected onto and through the stripe as it moves through the film projector sprockets. The beam, modulated by the dark and light patterns of the stripe, is picked up by a light-sensing photo-electric cell that translates the patterns into sound.

overtone part of the harmonic series higher than the fundamental frequency.

parabolic dish a bowl-shaped apparatus designed to focus and capture sound from a distance.

pitch often perceived as frequency but more subjective since it is dependent on both the loudness and timbre of the sound produced.

quiet   generally the absence of noise, often equated with silence.

quietude   a state of quiet and calm.

reverberation   repetitions of sound so closely spaced in time as not to be individually discernable. These phenomena occur in both indoor and outdoor environments.

riparian   habitats along the banks of rivers.

sample   to take all or part of a sound out of its original context so that it can be transformed into another context.

shock-mount   in audio terms, a microphone mounting system designed to attenuate and control for external vibrations that can affect the quality of recordings.

signal-to-noise   in recording, this is the ratio of "useful information," or signal (what is desirable to record), to unwanted noise (produced by recording electronics, or other background sound). If the signal is loud enough in relation to the noise, the noise will tend to be imperceptible.

silence   the complete absence of sound, a phenomenon rarely found in the natural world because such a habitat would likely not support life.

sonogram   a spectrogram.

soundscape   the total acoustic environment that we perceive in any given moment. It consists of three different sources of sound: geophony, biophony, and anthropophony.

soundscape ecology   a new discipline that contrasts with and incorporates older elements of study like landscape ecology, a discipline of observing landscape structures and systems that was first given expression in the late 1930s, and acoustic ecology, which came into the lexicon in the late 1970s through programs initiated by R. Murray Schafer and Barry Truax at Simon Fraser University in Vancouver. Soundscape ecology, the study of sound emanating from the landscape, assumes that natural soundscapes consist of a combination of both geophonies and biophonies. These sources, in combination, comprise an ongoing, profoundly informative narrative—the world's first bio- and geo-acoustic descriptive. Among other things, this articulation provides instant feedback as to how well humans are relating to their surrounding living environment through the multiple ways in which vocal organisms collectively express themselves.

sound sculpture   the sculpting of sound much as artists in any "hard" form (clay, metal, ceramic, etc.) do. The results, when commissioned to the fullest extent of our technical and production capabilities, are three-dimensional performances that fill anything from small rooms to very large spaces. Expressed in the pieces are textures (of a place), feelings of light and dark, negative and positive space, kinetics, color, form, tension and release, and, of course, content (location, concept, environment, day/night, spatial themes, etc.). Additionally, sound sculptures provide listeners with experiences that transport them to places otherwise impossible through the application of alternative media.

spectrogram   a graphic illustration of sound featuring time on one axis, frequency on another, and amplitude defined by light or dark gray-scale or color intensity of the image; also called a sonogram or a voice print.

spectrum   in audio, the ability of a device (ear, microphone, recorder, etc.) to detect or reproduce sound. Humans have the ability to hear a frequencies between 20 Hz and 20 kHz—this is the entire range of the human frequency spectrum. This is typically also defined as the normal range of reproducible sound in most professional and semiprofessional recording gear.

stereo   a class of recorded sounds that typically begins with two microphones (or one system with two mic elements) set in relation to each other so that the illusion of spatial information in the environment is captured. For the purposes of this document, it includes XY, M-S, and binaural recording.

timbre   the unique quality of a given voice or combination of voices that can signify the character of a particular bird, mammal, or amphibian, instrument in a human orchestra, combinations of instruments, or creature voices (see biophony). Sometimes this sound characteristic is referred to as tone color.

tone   usually referred to as the particular quality, characteristic, or color of a sound.

transducer   in recording, any device that either receives or transmits audio signals by converting one type of energy into another. These include microphones, hydrophones, headphones, and audio speakers.

tranquility   a state of serenity or calmness.

ultrasound   sounds higher in frequency (more than 20 kHz) than the human capacity to detect.

white noise   similar to the idea of white light, this is an audio signal that has equal power in any band of a given bandwidth (power spectral density) across the entire frequency spectrum when the bandwidth is measured in Hz.

XY   a form of stereo using two cardioid mics set in a specific relationship to each other.

Notes

Introduction

1. Bernie Krause, *Wild Soundscapes in the National Parks: An Educational Program Guide to Listening and Recording* (National Park Service, March 2002).

2. R. Murray Schafer, *The Book of Noise* (Indian River, Ontario: Arcana Editions, 1998).

3. S. J. Gould, "Abolish the Recent," *Natural History*, May 1991, pp. 16–21.

Chapter 1. The Mystery of Sound

1. E. H. Berger, L. H. Royster, J. D. Royster, D. P. Driscoll, and M. Layne, *The Noise Manual*, 5th edition (Fairfax, Va.: American Industrial Hygiene Association Press, 2000).

2. Bernie Krause, *Into a Wild Sanctuary* (Heyday Books, 1998); Bernie Krause, *The Great Animal Orchestra: Finding the Origins of Music in the World's Wild Places* (Boston: Little, Brown, 2012).

3. Janet Raloff, "Noise and Stress in Humans," *Science News* 121 (June 5, 1982): 380.

4. R. Murray Schafer, *Tuning of the World* (Toronto: McClelland and Stewart, 1977).

5. David Abram, *Awakening What's Wild Within Us* (Wild Earth, Milkweed Press, 2002).

6. Hermann Helmholtz, *On the Sensations of Tone* (reprint, Dover, 1954; originally published 1863).

7. Paul Shepard, *Coming Home to the Pleistocene* (Island Press, 1998).

Chapter 2. Stories Revealed by the Biophony

1. Verna R. Johnston, *Sierra Nevada: The Naturalist's Companion* (Berkeley: University of California Press, 1998).

2. Ken Marten and Peter Marler, "Sound Transmission and Its Significance for Animal Vocalization: I. Temperate Habitats," *Behavioral Ecology and Sociobiology* 2 (1977): 271–290.

3. Jakob von Uexküll, *Umwelt und Innenwelt der Tiere* (Berlin: J. Springer, 1909).

4. Bernie Krause, "Bio-acoustics: Habitat Ambience and Ecological Balance," *Whole Earth Review,* no. 57 (Winter, 1987): 14–15.

5. *The Nature of Sound,* Resource Manual #47, National Park Service, revised 1999.

6. S. C. Creel, J. E. Fox, A. Hardy, J. Sands, B. Garrott, and R. O. Peterson, "Snowmobile Activity and Glucocorticoid Stress Responses in Wild Wolves and Elk," *Conservation Biology* 16, no. 3 (June 2002): 809–814.

7. National Park Service, Director's Order #47: Soundscape Preservation and Noise Management, Robert Stanton, director, December 1, 2000 (http://www.nps.gov/refdesk/DOrders/DOrder47.html).

Chapter 3. Exploring Soundscapes

1. This list was compiled by Mike Mieszala, a teacher at Warren Township High School in Illinois, and his students for a Skype classroom interchange, November 7, 2014; used with permission.

2. Ambrose Bierce, *The Devil's Dictionary* (reprint, Dover, 1958; originally published 1911).

3. Don Kroodsma (text), Lang Elliott (pictures), *Surfing the Dawn* (1999, http://www.naturesound.com/kroods/kroods.html).

4. W. A. Mathieu, *The Listening Book* (Boston: Shambhala Publications, 1991).

5. M. A. Cooper, F. N. Kulstev, et al., "Direct and Sensitive Detection of a Human Virus by Rupture Event Scanning," *Nature* 19 (September 2001): 833–837.

Chapter 4. The Language of Soundscapes

1. Maurice Merleau-Ponty, *Signs* (Evanston, Ill.: Northwestern University Press, 1964).

2. R. Murray Schafer, *Once Upon a Windy Night,* CD (Grouse Records, Vancouver, 2000).

Chapter 5. The Art of Hearing and Recording

1. *Songs of the Humpback Whales,* recorded by Frank Watlington and Roger Payne, produced by Roger Payne (Columbia Records, 1968).

2. W. D. Ward, L. H. Royster, and J. D. Royster, "Anatomy and Physiology of the Ear: Normal and Damaged Hearing," *The Noise Manual,* ed. E. H. Berger et al., 5th edition (American Industrial Hygiene Association, 2000), 101–106.

Chapter 6. Equipment in a Nutshell

1. More detailed information can be found in the expert and straightforward *New Stereo Soundbook,* by Ron Streicher and F. Alton Everest, 2nd edition (Pasadena, Calif.: Audio Engineering Associates, 1998).

2. Good-quality mic systems of this type can be purchased for as little as two hundred dollars to more than eight thousand dollars. Some come equipped with battery-operated internal preamplifiers. Others—usually the more expensive ones— require an outboard preamplifier that can cost from six hundred to fifteen hundred dollars.

3. Lang Elliott, personal correspondence.

4. Sony ECM-957 PRO or ECM-680S, for instance.

5. For stereo playback of an M-S signal, the signal output is calculated and derived in the following way: M *plus* S for the left channel, and M *minus* S for the right output channel. The width and depth of the stereo image is continuously variable from mono. This is particularly useful since other stereo configurations (XY and binaural, for instance) can create up to a −3 dB signal drop in the phantom center channel whereas the M-S system eliminates this phenomenon (1 decibel, or dB, is the minimum level of change in amplitude the human ear can detect). The "phantom center" is an audio engineering expression which refers to the illusion of audio information appearing directly in the center between a pair of stereo speakers. The sound doesn't *actually* come from the center (there is no speaker there). It just sounds that way when the speakers and mix are balanced properly. With most stereo mic systems, the drop of level in the phantom center occurs because the patterns of the mics fail to cover information coming from that zone at the same level as the side perspectives.

Chapter 7. Dealing with Noise

1. Paul Shepard, *Nature and Madness* (University of Georgia Press, 1998).

2. "Tina Turner Aversion," *San Francisco Chronicle,* September 19, 1999.

3. *San Francisco Chronicle,* November 1997.

Chapter 9. While Listening and Recording

1. These, with a musical score by Phil Aaberg, can be heard on an album download called *Meridian* (http://wildstore.wildsanctuary.com/collections/music -albums/products/meridian-a-journey-of-spring).

2. A mono-compatible, near coincident array of microphones designed to give highly localized stereo imaging for loudspeaker reproduction; Ron Streicher and F. Alton Everest, *The New Stereo Soundbook,* 2nd edition (Pasadena, Calif.: Audio Engineering Associates, 1998).

3. Songmeter SM3, by Wildlife Acoustics (http://www.wildlifeacoustics .com/products/song-meter-sm3).

Chapter 10. Archiving and Creating Projects

1. *Sampling* means taking all or parts of a sound out of its original context, usually so that it can be placed in another. Also, recording a sound into a musical instrument sampler in order to play it back with different pitches or durations.

Chapter 11. Recording Production Techniques

1. *Midsummer Nights* (http://wildstore.wildsanctuary.com/collections /soundscape-albums/products/midsummer-nights); *Antarctica* (http://wildstore .wildsanctuary.com/collections/soundscape-albums/products/antarctica).

Chapter 12. Bioregions and Sounds to Explore

1. *Desert Solitudes* (http://wildstore.wildsanctuary.com/collections/sound scape-albums/products/desert-solitudes).

2. *Death Valley Oasis* (http://wildstore.wildsanctuary.com/collections/sound scape-albums/products/death-valley-oasis).

3. Click on "Research," then "Articles," then on the paper titled "Loss of Natural Soundscape: Global Implications of Its Effect on Humans and Other Creatures."

4. Matthew A. Cooper et al., "Direct and Sensitive Detection of a Human Virus by Rupture Event Scanning," *Nature Biotechnology* 18 (September 2001): 833–837.

5. *Winds Across the Tundra* (http://wildstore.wildsanctuary.com/collections /soundscape-albums/products).

6. *Voice of the Arctic Refuge* (http://wildstore.wildsanctuary.com/collections /soundscape-albums/products/voice-of-the-arctic-refuge).

Bibliography

Abbey, Edward, *Down the River,* E. P. Dutton, 1982.

Abram, David, *The Spell of the Sensuous,* Pantheon, 1996.

Berendt, Joachim-Ernst, *The Third Ear,* Owl Books, Henry Holt & Co., 1992.

Carson, Rachel, *Silent Spring,* Houghton Mifflin Co., 1962.

Chatwin, Bruce, *Songlines,* Penguin Books, 1987.

Eiseley, Loren, *The Night Country,* Scribners, 1971.

——, *The Unexpected Universe,* Harcourt Brace, 1994.

Elliott, Lang, *A Guide to Wildlife Sounds: The Sounds of 100 Mammals, Birds, Reptiles, Amphibians, and Insects,* Stackpole Books, 2005.

——, *Common Birds and Their Songs,* Houghton Mifflin Harcourt, Pap/Com edition (October 6, 1998).

Feld, Steven, *Sound and Sentiment: Birds, Weeping, Poetics, and Song in Kaluli Expression,* Temple University Press, 1991.

Keizer, Garrett, *The Unwanted Sound of Everything We Want: A Book About Noise,* PublicAffairs, reprint edition (March 13, 2012).

Krause, B. L., *Notes from the Wild,* Ellipsis Arts, 1996.

——, *Into a Wild Sanctuary,* Heyday Books, 1998.

——, *The Great Animal Orchestra: Finding the Origins of Music in the World's Wild Places,* Little, Brown/Hachette, 2012.

——, *Voices of the Wild: Animal Songs, Human Din, and the Call to Save Natural Soundscapes,* Yale University Press, 2015.

Louv, Richard, *Last Child in the Woods: Saving Our Children from Nature Deficit Disorder,* Algonquin Books, updated and expanded edition (April 10, 2008).

Lyon, Thomas, "Noise and the Sacred," *Utah Wilderness Association Review,* May/June 1995.

Mathieu, W. A., *The Listening Book: Discovering Your Own Music,* Shambhala Press, 1991.

———, *A Musical Life,* Shambhala Press, 1994.

Sarno, Louis, *The Extraordinary Music of the Babenzélé Pygmies,* Ellipsis Arts, 1996.

Schafer, R. Murray, *Tuning of the World,* Destiny Books, 1977.

———, *Voices of Tyranny: Temples of Silence,* Arcana Editions, 1993.

———, *The Book of Noise,* Arcana Editions, 1998.

Shepard, Paul, *The Others: How Animals Made Us Human,* Island Press, 1996.

———, *Nature & Madness,* Sierra Club Books, 1982.

Streicher, Ron, and F. Alton Everest, *The New Stereo Review,* 2nd edition, Audio Engineering Associates, Pasadena, California, 1998.

Wilson, E. O., *Biodiversity,* National Academy Press, Washington, D.C., 1988.

Wiseman, Alan, *The World Without Us,* Picador, reprint edition (August 5, 2008).

Acknowledgments

Grateful acknowledgment is extended to the following writers and publishers for allowing me to quote from their work.

p. 29   Hermann Hesse, "Sometimes," from *News from the Universe: Poems of Twofold Consciousness,* Robert Bly, translator and ed. (San Francisco: Sierra Club Books, 1980); reprinted in *Earth Prayers from Around the World,* Elizabeth Roberts and Elias Amidon, eds. (HarperSanFrancisco, a division of HarperCollins Publishers, 1991).

p. 65   Gabon Pygmy, Africa, "All Lives, All Dances, & All is Loud," from *Technicians of the Sacred: A Range of Poetries from Africa, America, Asia, Europe, and Oceania,* 2nd edition, Jerome Rothenberg, ed. (Berkeley: University of California Press, 1968, 1985). Permission graciously given by Jerome Rothenberg.

p. 70   José Emilio Pacheco, "Defense and Illustration of Poetry," from *An Ark for the Next Millennium: Poems by José Emilio Pacheco,* translations by Margaret Sayers Peden; selections by Jorge Esquinca (Austin: University of Texas Press, 1993).

p. 73   Marcia Falk, "Listen," from *The Book of Blessings* (HarperSanFrancisco, 1996; paperback edition, Beacon Press, 1999), copyright © 1996 by Marcia Lee Falk. Used by permission of author.

p. 73   Orpingalik, a Netsilik Eskimo, a statement from *Technicians of the Sacred,* cited above.

p. 177 Aboriginal from Arnhem Land, Australia, a poem from *Technicians of the Sacred,* cited above.

p. 180 William Butler Yeats, "The Lake Isle of Innisfree," from *The Yeats Reader,* Richard J. Finneran, ed. (New York: Scribner Poetry, © 1997 by Anne Yeats).

p. 214 Gary Lawless, "When the Animals Come to Us," from *Earth Prayers from Around the World,* cited above; first published in *First Sight of Land* (Nobelboro, Minn.: Blackberry Books). Permission graciously given by the author.

To Jannie Dresser, who recognized early on the value of the messages and helped structure the original narrative; to Martyn Stewart and Dan Dugan, teachers extraordinare, for their incredible insights about and support for this work, in general, for imparting to others the skills they need to know in order to become effective in the field, and for their advice and rigorous efforts to keep me honest, on message and on track; to the soundscape community that has grown from fewer than a dozen participants when I began nearly fifty years ago to a worldwide collaboration of thousands; to the reviewers who lent their expertise and helpful comments to the message, and to my editors, Joe Calamia and Phillip King. Most prominently to my dear wife, Katherine, to whom all gratitude is due. And to Gillian MacKenzie, my thoughtful and proactive agent who knows where the wonders lie.

Index

Page numbers in italic type refer to illustrations

211